CONTENTS

Ships in Focus Publications

Correspondence and editorial:
Roy Fenton
18 Durrington Avenue
London SW20 8NT
020 8879 3527
record@rfenton.co.uk

Orders and photographic:
John & Marion Clarkson
18 Franklands, Longton
Preston PR4 5PD
01772 612855
shipsinfocus@btinternet.com

© 2014 Individual contributors,
John Clarkson and Roy Fenton.

Printed by Amadeus Press Ltd.,
Cleckheaton, Yorkshire.
Designed by Hugh Smallwood, John Clarkson
and Roy Fenton.

**SHIPS IN FOCUS RECORD
ISBN 978-0-9928263-0-7**

SUBSCRIPTION RATES FOR RECORD

Readers can start their subscription with any
issue, and are welcome to backdate it to receive
previous issues.

	3 issues	4 issues
UK	£27	£35
Europe (airmail)	£29	£38
Rest of the world (surface mail)	£29	£38
Rest of the world (airmail)	£35	£46

SHIPS IN FOCUS

Marc

We have not increased the price o
For the last 22 editions, we have worked hard to minimise our
costs, largely by producing ourselves the artwork for each issue,
and scanning all the photographs used (avoiding, we trust, any
diminution of quality). Short of buying our own printing works,
we have now exhausted ways of fighting cost increases, and have
no option but to increase the price of 'Record', and from this issue
it will cost £8.50. We regret the need for a price rise, but still
believe the 64 pages of each 'Record' offer excellent value for
money. Needless to say, subscribers who are still in credit will not
be charged the new price until their renewal becomes due.

We would remind readers that subscribing to three or
more editions offers a significant saving, and subscribers can also
purchase new Ships in Focus publications at favourable prices.
After a lean year in 2013, this year we are expecting a bumper
crop of books, starting with 'Rix Shipping', advertised elsewhere
in this issue. Our programme also includes 'Blue Star Line: a
Fleet History', which we believe will offer the definitive history of
all the ships owned and chartered by this iconic and much missed
company, together with a wealth of photographs, an account of the
Line's fortunes, and reminiscences of working for Blue Star.

The Index to articles and ships in 'Records' 1 to 56
mentioned in our last editorial was completed a few months
ago and copies of the CD have been shipped to those who
have ordered them. Compiling it required a lengthy process of
checking and cross-referencing the ships that were listed, as many
appear more than once in the 56 issues. We were interested to
find that there are entries for no less than 17,000 individual ships
which have been referred to in 'Record'. The CD has 27 files in
Microsoft Word format, one for the index of articles and 26 for the
ships themselves. Using Word files mean that it is easy for users
to search the index of articles for any word in the title of an article,
so that very little cross indexing has been necessary. Copies of
the Index CD are available from our London address for £2.50,
a bargain price given the amount of work entailed, maintains the
main compiler, Heather Fenton.

John Clarkson   Roy Fenton

Mékong was the first ship in the post-war rebuilding programme of
Messageries Maritimes, as described from page 2 onwards. *[World Ship
Society Ltd.]*

Built just four years earlier, *Norwich Trader* (2) was transferred from General Steam in 1948 (top). *[Fotoflite incorporating Skyfotos/ Roy Fenton collection]*

Lynn Trader, acquired in 1951, was something of a liability, and despite investment in new machinery proved too slow for the Great Yarmouth company's services (middle). *[Fotoflite incorporating Skyfotos/ Roy Fenton collection]*

One of a number of Dutch motor coasters considered for purchase in 1955, *Betty* is seen at Preston (left). *[Harry Stewart/J. and M. Clarkson collection]*

Yarmouth Trader was another second-hand acquisition, this time from Hull Gates Shipping Co. Ltd. (opposite page). *[Fotoflite incorporating Skyfotos/ J. and M. Clarkson collection]*

GREAT YARMOUTH SHIPPING CO. LTD.
Part 2
Roy Fenton

Ships and lighters began returning from requisition in October 1945. It was now decided to dispose of most of the older steamers, and they were gradually sold, often yielding modest profits considering their age. Release of *Yellowhammer* was delayed until September 1947, but she had been reconditioned at government expense, allowing the company to sell her almost immediately to W.N. Lindsay of Leith for a handsome £11,500. This helped boost profits for the year sufficient for the board to declare a 10% dividend.

Some claims for recompense dragged on for many years. A continuing theme of board minutes was pursuing a claim for damage to the Continental Wharf at Yarmouth during its wartime use by the Admiralty. Not until 1950 was this settled, and then only for £2,796 although reinstatement of the wharf had cost the company £15,000. Despite these difficulties, the immediate post-war period saw the company's services prospering.

To replace the ageing steamers newer motor vessels were bought, including General Steam's *Mallard* which became *Norwich Trader*. But board minutes warn that the company could no longer count on General Steam to meet its tonnage replacement needs, as the parent company was itself in an 'acute tonnage position'. The next acquisitions came from elsewhere, including the relatively modern motor ship *Friargate* bought in 1950 to become *Yarmouth Trader*. A less impressive coaster acquired in 1951 was the *Helen Fairplay*. She had been laid down in wartime as the tanker *Chant 40* but completed as a dry cargo vessel when it was decided that the Normandy invasion did not require as many tankers as was originally thought. Her modest acquisition price of £16,500 reflected her acute need for re-engining, new machinery being ordered for

£10,500. Even then, *Lynn Trader* as she had become was not considered a good buy, her ungainly hull making her speed unsatisfactory. Having previously managed one of these ugly craft, *Empire Farringdon*, the company should not have been surprised at this problem. Notwithstanding these expenses, a leap in profits allowed the dividend to be increased to 15% in 1952 and to 25% in 1953.

Further fleet replacements were regarded as urgent in 1955, and several foreign motor coasters were considered, including the German *Antwerpen* (497/1953), and the Dutch ships *Betty* (400/1951) and *Jell* (396/1955). However, a sudden upturn in freight rates, particularly in the Baltic timber trades, saw these either withdrawn from sale or snapped up by other purchasers. The Dutch *Arbon* was on time charter to the company, and she was acquired in July 1956 to become *Norfolk Trader*. She was to be the last ship bought, signalling a change in the fortunes of the company which now began a struggle for survival.

Slow decline

Although a dividend of 20% was paid in 1957, troubles were mounting with a worsening trading position and an ageing fleet - the 23-year-old *Lowestoft Trader* requiring heavy repairs. It was increasingly difficult to find remunerative cargoes for the ships that were tramping, and it was necessary to lay up *Yarmouth Trader* and *Lynn Trader* at Yarmouth. *Boston Trader* was found employment on General Steam's services to the River Rhine. *Norwich Trader* and *Lowestoft Trader* were sufficient to deal with the Rotterdam and Antwerp services, and a sign of boardroom unease was that it was felt imperative to 'eliminate unprofitable tramp voyages' and to 'engage in active canvassing for cargoes'.

In an initiative to increase business, a weekly service between Felixstowe and Harlingen was opened by *Lowestoft Trader* in September 1958. It did not prove particularly remunerative, as the only cargo to be had was strawboard carried inward, and for several months no outward cargoes could be found. Extension of the service to Rotterdam, Antwerp and eventually Amsterdam followed, with General Steam's *Fauvette* (592/1935) chartered in, and the *Lowestoft Trader* redeployed on the Rhine services of the parent company. Much of the board's time over ensuing months was taken up with discussion of how to make this additional service pay, and calls at Boston were added, only for expenses there to prove higher than anticipated. Eventually it was conceded that what cargoes were available could be handled with calls by just one service between Felixstowe and Dordrecht. In 1960 General Steam considered opening a service between Ipswich and Rotterdam, but were concerned that this would adversely impact on the Great Yarmouth company's Yarmouth to Rotterdam trade.

Seen on the Thames on 1st June 1953, General Steam's *Fauvette* was chartered by the Great Yarmouth company in the late 1950s. *[J. and M. Clarkson collection]*

Problems extended to local operations. Late in 1959 Stephenson Clarke notified the company that its coal shipments for Norwich Gas Works via Yarmouth would cease at the end of the year. This made most of the Great Yarmouth company's remaining fleet of lighters and tugs redundant, and all but two lighters were laid up at Norwich or Yarmouth until sold or scrapped.

These difficulties were reflected in a rapidly worsening financial performance. Profits which allowed dividends of 20% to be paid in 1956 and 1957 fell dramatically in 1958, although it was still considered appropriate to pay a 10% dividend. It was to be the last such payment: a loss of almost £15,000 ensued in 1959, growing to nearly £28,000 in 1960. Although losses were limited to more reasonable figures through most of the 1960s, the

company was obviously in terminal decline. By 1963 it was facing 'very serious competition' from the twice-weekly service of the Norfolk Line. Subsidiary T. Small and Co. Ltd. was still trading profitably, and presumably it was this, plus the Great Yarmouth company's wharves and other terminal facilities, that persuaded General Steam to keep the company going, despite there being little prospect of turning round the shipping business. When Yarmouth became an important base for servicing the oil and gas installations in the southern North Sea, the facilities in the port were valuable, and they eventually became part of the offshore activities of P&O, General Steam's parent.

The Great Yarmouth company's ships gradually followed the inland craft in being sold, often for minimal prices reflecting their age (the company managed the not inconsiderable feat of never selling a ship to breakers). As replacements, motor ships were chartered in: from the General Steam parent came *Peregrine* (890/1941) and *Mavis* (381/1946) in 1961, and *Kingfisher* (493/1944) in 1964; whilst Dutch and German coasters gradually came to be preferred, *Nomadische* (363/1951) chartered in 1965, and *Jurgen Drews* (496/1957) and *Herm-S* (425/1954) in 1967. Oddly, by 1966 the liner services out of Yarmouth were in the hands of chartered Dutch coasters, whilst their last surviving owned ship, *Norfolk Trader* – a Dutch coaster herself but of an earlier period – was bare-boat chartered to General Steam.

General Steam took over the Felixstowe route in May 1965, whilst services from Yarmouth to Rotterdam continued until April 1969, the last ship departing

Chartered to Great Yarmouth in 1961 as its own ships were sold, *Mavis* is seen in General Steam colours on 21st June 1953. *[J. and M. Clarkson]*

General Steam's *Kingfisher* (above) was chartered to the company in 1964, and may well be in Great Yarmouth colours here, as the white line on the hull follows the shape of the bulwarks, rather than following the sheer line as it did in General Steam vessels. The paint scheme emphasises the angular lines of this war-built coaster [Ships in Focus]

The Dutch motor coaster *Nomadisch* (right) was chartered by the Great Yarmouth company in 1965. [J. and M. Clarkson]

Rotterdam on the third of the month. Great Yarmouth's agents, Comar Shipping and Trading Co. Ltd., decided to continue sailings using the company's wharf at Yarmouth, and were even considering containerisation, something the Great Yarmouth company had first considered ten years earlier but had never acted on. Nevertheless, the route closed in February 1970, the month that coincidentally also saw the sale of Great Yarmouth's last ship, *Norfolk Trader*. The ABC Wharf at Yarmouth carried on in use, hired to a company running a service to Gibraltar, and there was some warehousing, but this was insufficient to justify the company continuing in existence. The last board meeting and the last AGM were held in February 1971, and trading ceased in October 1972 when the company's remaining assets and liabilities were transferred to T. Small and Co. Ltd.

The Great Yarmouth Shipping Co. Ltd. was throughout its fifty-year life effectively a subsidiary of the General Steam Navigation Co. Ltd., although it inherited some board members and officers from its other constituents. General Steam's financial interest increased in stages and from 1946 the parent company consolidated its interest by providing its Chairman, after which the Great Yarmouth company is referred to as a 'wholly-owned subsidiary' of General Steam, although shareholding did not alter at this date. Despite this and much interchange of ships with its parent, Great Yarmouth Shipping Co. Ltd. achieved considerable independence and besides its own fleet of ships and river craft had a sufficient interest in wharves and other facilities in Norfolk to be regarded as a local company, serving businesses in Yarmouth and Norwich.

Fleet list part 2

13. NORWICH TRADER (2) 1948-1965

O.N. 169942 377g 167n.
143.5 x 6.1 x 9.1 feet.
2SCSA 7-cyl. oil engine by Crossley Brothers Ltd., Manchester.
6.7.1944: Launched by Henry Scarr Ltd., Hessle (Yard No. 434).
8.1944: Completed for the General Steam Navigation Co. Ltd., London as MALLARD.
1948: Transferred to the Great Yarmouth Shipping Co. Ltd., Yarmouth for £38,500 and renamed NORWICH TRADER.
7.10.1965: Sold to G. &. E. Zervas, Thessaloniki, Greece for £12,000 and renamed NIKOLAOS.
1972: Sold to E. Kallikis & E. Efstathiou, Thessaloniki.
1978: Resold to G. &. E. Zervas, Thessaloniki.
1988: Broken up at Aliaga, Turkey.

14. YARMOUTH TRADER (2) 1950-1959

O.N. 181201 945g 503n.
202.6 x 31.4 x 12.0 feet.
2SCSA 6-cyl. oil engine by the Newbury Diesel Co. Ltd., Newbury.
22.12.1945: Launched by the Goole Shipbuilding and Repairing Co. Ltd., Goole (Yard No 427).
3.1946: Completed for the Hull Gates Shipping Co. Ltd. (Craggs and Jenkins Ltd., managers), Hull as FRIARGATE.
1950: Acquired by the Great Yarmouth Shipping Co. Ltd., Yarmouth for £83,500 and renamed YARMOUTH TRADER.
20.7.1959: Sold to G. Stergiopoulos, Piraeus, Greece for £21,250 and renamed PROTOPOROS.
1960: Sold to John Stewart and Co. (Shipping) Ltd., Glasgow and renamed YEWCROFT.
1965: Sold to Kontos Brothers, Piraeus, Greece and renamed GEORGIOS KONTOS.
1971: Renamed PANAGHIA.
19.10.1971: Sank south of Cape Gata, Cyprus in position 34.27 north by 33.10 east whilst on a voyage from Marina di Carrara, Italy to Beirut with a cargo of 1,050 tons of marble blocks. The crew of ten were taken off by the Greek motor vessel PELIAS (1,189/1955) which attempted unsuccessfully to tow PANAGHIA before she sank.

Norwich Trader (2) in the Thames. *[Ships in Focus]*

Yarmouth Trader. *[World Ship Society Ltd.]*

Yarmouth Trader was unusual in going to a Greek owner, then returning to British registry. She is seen as *Yewcroft*, a name carried from 1960 to 1965, after which she returned to the Greek flag.*[FototoFlite incorporating Skyfotos BWB819]*

15. LYNN TRADER (2) 1951-1960

O.N. 180370 404g 184n.

142.2 x 27.0 x 8.5 feet.

2SCSA 6-cyl. oil engine by Petters Ltd., Loughborough.

1953: 2SCSA 4-cyl. oil engine by British Polar Engines Ltd., Glasgow.

16.12.1944: Launched by the Goole Shipbuilding and Repairing Co. Ltd., Goole (Yard No. 433). She had been laid down as CHANT 40, later becoming FABRIC 40 on the decision to complete her not as a tanker but as a dry cargo vessel.

1.1945: Completed for the Minister of War Transport, London (R. Hunt and Sons, Hull, managers) as EMPIRE FAIRPLAY.

1949: Sold to Overseas Fish Import Co. Ltd., Yarmouth and renamed HELEN FAIRPLAY.

1951: Acquired by the Great Yarmouth Shipping Co. Ltd., Yarmouth for £16,500 and renamed LYNN TRADER.

1953: Re-engined.

22.6.1960: Sold to Fouad Hassan Hamza, Port Said, Egypt for £15,040 and renamed HAMZA I.

1997: Deleted from 'Lloyd's Register' as continued existence in doubt.

16. NORFOLK TRADER 1956-1970

O.N. 187905 455g 227n.

164.5 x 27.8 x 10.7 feet.

4SCSA. 6-cyl. oil engine by Motorenfabriek 'De Industrie', Alphen an der Rhein, Netherlands.

16.12.1953: Launched by D. & J. Boot 'De Industrie', Alphen an der Rhein (Yard No. 1229).

1954: Completed for N.V. 'Fegro' (Holschers Kustvaart Bedrijf N.V., managers), Dordrecht, Netherlands as ARBON.

14.7.1956: Acquired by the Great Yarmouth Shipping Co. Ltd., Yarmouth and renamed NORFOLK TRADER.

4.2.1970: Sold to A. Zafeiroudis, Thessaloniki, Greece for £14,500 and renamed CHRISTOFOROS.

1976: Renamed PHILLIPOS K.

1983: Renamed DIANA D.

23.11.1983: Sank following a collision with the US Navy landing ship FORT SNELLING 20 miles off Sidon and 35 miles south west of Beirut. She was on a voyage from Vassiliko to Sidon with a cargo of cement. The crew was rescued.

Lynn Trader. [Ships in Focus]

The last ship owned by the Great Yarmouth Shipping Company, the Dutch coaster *Arbon* (above) was renamed *Norfolk Trader* (below) on acquisition in 1956. *[Both J. and M. Clarkson]*

Managed for the Ministry of War Transport.

M1. EMPIRE DAFFODIL 1940-1946

O.N. 167513 398g 112n.
180.3 x 27.8 x 7.6 feet.
4SCSA 7-cyl. oil engine by Klockner-Humboldt-Deutz A.G., Koln, Germany.

3.1940: Completed by Scheepsvaart Gebroeder van Diepen N.V., Waterhuizen, Netherlands (Yard No 841) for S.G. Hallström, Stockholm as CARIBE II, but not delivered. She had been laid down for Compania Anonima de Navegacion del Caribe, Caracas, Venezuela.

1940: Requisitioned by the Ministry of War Transport, London (Great Yarmouth Shipping Co. Ltd., Yarmouth, managers) and renamed EMPIRE DAFFODIL.

9.7.1940: Damaged by air attack south west of the Isle of Wight. Taken to Portland and then to Southampton for repair.

1946: Sold to the General Steam Navigation Co. Ltd., London, and renamed GREENFINCH.

1966: Sold to G.M. Moundreas and Brothers, Piraeus, Greece and renamed MOIRA.

1966: Sold to Orri Navigation Lines, Jeddah, and renamed STAR OF MEDINA.

11.1993: Deleted from 'Lloyd's Register' as continued existence in doubt.

M2. DRITTURA 1940-1945

187g 112n 104.9 x 20.5 x 8.1 feet.
4SCSA 3-cyl.oil engine by
N.V. Appingedammer Brons Motorenfabriek, Appingedammer, Netherlands; 8.5 knots.

21.3.1929: Completed by Scheepsbouw- & Reparatiewerf J. Vos & Zoon, Groningen, Netherlands (Yard No. 64) for Derk Roelof Kajuiter, Groningen as DRITTURA .

16.5.1940: Taken over by the Netherlands Shipping and Trading Committee, London, with aspects of management entrusted to Great Yarmouth Shipping Co. Ltd., Yarmouth.

1.6.1945: Returned to owners.

7.3.1957: Sold to Klaas van der Veen, Groningen.

13.2.1969: Sold to Gerrit van Rosevelt, Capelle aan den Ijssel, Netherlands and converted into a yacht at Harlingen.

29.1.1994: Sold to B.V. Store Baelt (V. Roos & J. Baayen), Monnickendam, Netherlands and renamed STORE BAELT.

No further details.

Managed from 1940 to 1946 by the Great Yarmouth company, the Dutch-built *Empire Daffodil* was owned by General Steam from 1946 to 1966, and is seen here as *Greenfinch* in May 1953 *[J. and M. Clarkson]*

Following wartime management, *Drittura* was returned to her Dutch owners in 1945, and is seen arriving at Whitstable. *[Charles Traill]*

Another war-managed Dutch coaster, *Deneb* was photographed off Woolwich, August 1955. *[J. and M. Clarkson]*

M3. DENEB 1940-1945

199g 110n 263d

113.2 (o.l.) 105.9 x 21.8 x 7.8 feet.

4SCSA 4-cyl. oil engine by
Apppingedammer Brons Motorenfabriek
N.V., Appingedam, Netherlands; 44 NHP.

1948: 2SCSA 6-cyl. oil engine by General
Motors Corporation, Detroit, USA.

11.1950: 2SCSA 4-cyl. oil engine by N.V.
Machinefabriek Bolnes, Bolnes, Netherlands.

1928: Completed by Gebroeder G. and
H. Bodewes, Hasselt, Netherlands for L.
Veldman (D. Oosting, manager), Delfzijl,
Netherlands as HARRY.

1933: Renamed DENEB

1938: Sold to H. Salomons, Groningen,
Netherlands.

4.6.1940: Taken over by the Netherlands
Shipping and Trading Committee, London,
with aspects of management entrusted to
Great Yarmouth Shipping Co. Ltd., Yarmouth.

29.8.1945: Returned to owner.

1956: Sold to J. Stam and J. Dijken (N.V.
Scheepvaartbedrijf 'Poseidon', Delfzijl,
managers) and renamed PAX.

1960: Owner became J. Dijken (Beck's
Scheepvaartkantoor N.V, Groningen,
managers) and renamed LUCTOR.

1966: Sold to Société Anonyme Carbo-
Centre, Cormery, France and converted to a
sand carrier.

1971: Renamed YVES MICHÉLE.

1997: Deleted by 'Lloyd's Register' as
continued existence in doubt.

M4. EMPIRE FARRINGDON 1944-1948

O.N. 180293 411g 190n.

142.2 x 27.0 x 8.0 feet.

4SCSA 6-cyl. oil engine by Mirrlees,
Bickerton and Day Ltd., Stockport.

8.1960: 2SCSA 4-cyl. oil engine by Crossley
Brothers Ltd., Manchester.

8.1944: Launched by Henry Scarr Ltd.,
Hessle (Yard No. 450).

She had been laid down as CHANT 18, and
was later known as FABRIC 18.

9.1944: Completed for the Ministry of
War Transport, London (Great Yarmouth
Shipping Co. Ltd., Yarmouth, managers) as
EMPIRE FARRINGDON.

1946: Sold to De Malglaive Shipping Ltd.,
Windsor, Ontario and renamed SUSAN
OLIVIER.

1948: Sold to the Booker Line Ltd. (Booker
McConnell and Co. Ltd.), Liverpool.

1952: Renamed MABIRI.

8.1960: Re-engined.

1972: Sold to Island Shipping Co. Ltd.,
Trinidad.

19.2.1974: Sprang a leak 94 miles south
east of Tobago. Taken in tow but sank in
the Gulf of Paria in position 10.37 north by
61.34 west.

The one-time managed *Empire Farringdon* became *Susan Olivier* from 1946 to 1948. *[Fotoflite incorporating Skyfotos/Roy Fenton collection].*

Owned by Henry Colville/T. Small and Co. (Great Yarmouth) Ltd.

SAINT TUDWAL 1925-1929

O.N. 101756 198g 108n.

115.0 x 20.5 x 8.8 feet.

C. 2-cyl. by J.P. Rennoldson and Sons, South
Shields.

9.1895: Completed by C.S. Swan and
Hunter, Wallsend (Yard No.204) for Thomas
Lewis, Bangor as SAINT TUDWAL.

2.1909: Sold to the Bristol and Cardigan

Trading Co. Ltd. (Richard Thomas,
manager), Cardigan.

10.1915: Sold to William J. Duncan and
William A. Leith, Aberdeen.

10.1917: Sold to John J. Murphy, Waterford.

12.1922: Sold to Edward Caple and John
M. Beynon, Barry Dock.

3.1925: Acquired by Henry I. Colville
(Frederick Spashett, manager), Lowestoft.

1.1927: Transferred to T. Small and Co.
(Great Yarmouth) Ltd., Great Yarmouth.

11.1929: Sold to Stanley Harding, London.

9.1932: Sold to Francis J. Jordan,
Southampton.

5.1933: Sold to Alexander Johnston
(Samuel Gray, manager), Kilroot, Antrim.

12.8.1934: Struck Carraig Mhor Point,
Sound of Islay after she refused to answer
her helm when a steering chain had carried
away. She came off when put astern and
proceeded on her voyage, but made water
so fast that her pump could not cope and she
was abandoned by her crew and sank two
and a half miles and 84 degrees off Texa
Island. Her crew got ashore safely. She was
on a voyage from Goole to Londonderry
with a cargo of coal.

River craft known to have been owned	
Aphis	Lighter
Basswood	Lighter
Boxwood	Lighter
Carnelian	Lighter
Cedar	Lighter
Cypress	Steam tug
Ebony	Lighter
Fir	Wherry
Garnet	Lighter
Gensteam	Steam tug
Greenheart	Lighter
Hickory	Lighter
Jarrah	Lighter
Jenny Hope	Tug
Larch	Lighter
Nitter	Lighter
Opal	Steam wherry
Oulton	Lighter
Plane	Wherry
Purpleheart	Lighter
Quartz	Lighter
Queen	Lighter
Ruby	Lighter
Silver Birch	Lighter
Spruce	Lighter
Sumac	Lighter
Topaz	Lighter
Twenty	Lighter

The locally-built steam tugs *Cypress* (32/1930) (above) and *Gensteam* (31/1924) (below) were used on the Yare and other East Anglian waterways for towing lighters, often carrying coal from Yarmouth to the Norwich Gas Works, until this trade stopped in 1959. *[Both: P.A. Vicary/J. and M. Clarkson collection]*

BOSUN'S LOCKER - continued from pages 55/57

57/3

Has anyone any ideas on the identity of this ship? Looking at the forward part of the hull the paintwork gives the impression she has been on fire yet the white paintwork on the accommodation, both midships and aft, appears to be in good order. The bridge has gone and also the lifeboats. Her distinctive arrangement of masts and kingposts may be a clue. Being so low in the water one must asume she is sinking. *[J. and M. Clarkson collection]*

MESSAGERIES MARITIMES AND THEIR POST-WAR REBUILDING PROGRAMME

Part 1

Dr Jean-Pierre Burel

Some years ago, I published in these columns a letter commenting on the origins of the Messageries Maritimes. The post-Second World War period seemed an interesting choice for a follow-up.

Entrée en matière

From their creation in 1851, the Messageries Nationales, then Messageries Impériales, were always intimately linked to the French state. This period coincided with the start of France's colonial adventure, the building of the Empire, which implied the need to support troops overseas. In this regard the Crimean War served as a test case, with steam ships relentlessly towing sail transports to the Eastern Mediterranean. Another factor was the cutting of the Suez Canal, which shortened routes to the Far East and the Indian subcontinent.

Messageries Maritimes covered the Mediterranean as far as Alexandria, Jaffa and Beyrouth. West African trade was already under the control of British companies and of the powerful Fabre family, with its two associated lines, Chargeurs Reunis and Frayssinet. But the Algerian conquest, and the progressive takeover of Algerian services by another offshoot of France's Second Empire, Compagnie Générale Transatlantique, left the then Messageries Impériales looking for new destinations, a move begun in the thirty years which separated the start of the Algerian conquest from the Suez adventure.

The situation clearly called for a bold move towards the Far East with branch services to those coveted islands in the Indian Ocean, La Reunion (Ile Bourbon), Mauritius, and Madagascar. In the 1870s core services were directed towards China and Japan, with branch lines from Aden to the islands. In 1885, under a mail service convention, an independent service was established towards Australia, again with a branch service extending to New Caledonia and Tahiti.

The 1885 Indo-Chinese campaign conducted by Admiral Courbet, under the powerful lead of Jules Ferry, soon meant that the Messageries Maritimes were a cardinal stone in the building of colonies, carrying troops, civil servants, teachers and Christian missionaries. Of course, passenger services on such long hauls could not pay for themselves: mail subsidies were always necessary, and came under strict scrutiny from Parliament, leading to the 25-year 1887 convention which halved the total amount of money given to the company. This meant that fleet renewal was impossible, the company having to find resources from the lucrative cargo trade to Cochin-China, which came to absorb most of its resources for new buildings, and led to the sale of the wholely-owned La Ciotat yard.

In fact, this was the start of a bitter feud between Messageries and the French state, with a protracted court case which was still not settled by the end of the First World War. Thus, when it came up for renewal in 1912, the 1887 convention was simply extended on a yearly basis, in exchange for which Messageries could abandon its loss-making services: this is the origin of Compagnie Sud-Atlantique. Two flagships intended for this service went instead to the Far East service, *Paul Lecat* and *Andre Lebon*.

The year 1920 finally marked the end of the 1887 convention. The fleet had been bled by war (540 dead in the *Djemnah* torpedoing alone) and most units were long past their renewal date. Worse, the company was in no financial condition to rebuild: with France

The 1914-built *Andre Lebon* was damaged in an Allied air raid on Toulon in March 1944 and later scuttled by the retreating Germans. Remaining upright, she was quickly raised in May 1945 and re-entered Messagerie Maritimes' Far East service in October 1946 with little modification. After just six years she was withdrawn and was broken up in December 1952. *[Ian J. Farquhar collection]*

The *Djemnah* of 1874 was torpedoed by the German submarine *UB 105* south of Crete on 14th July 1918 when carrying over one thousand troops from Marseilles to Madagascar. Although in convoy, and escorted by HMS *Mallow*, barely half her complement were rescued. *[Ian J. Farquhar collection]*

on the verge of bankruptcy subsidies were at best scarce. The injection of seized German tonnage only temporarily plugged the void.

Again the French state intervened, separating the freight services as a completely private entity which soon fell under Chargeurs Réunis' control, and created the Services Contractuels des Messageries Maritimes, a state-run concern, using both the name of the old Messageries Maritime and its crews. This arrangement lasted until requisition by Direction des Transports Maritimes during the Second World War.

Occupation and Liberation

The Second World War more or less swept the fleet from the oceans. At home were occupying forces which, through the infamous 1942 Laval-Kaufman agreement, allocated most of the French merchant marine present in the Mediterranean to the Germans without counter payment: a silent tribute to the efforts of the unrestricted submarine warfare which the Royal Navy had run against the Italians. Those ships which tried to re-establish the vital link with the colonies were either seized by British forces off the Cape, Freetown or Gibraltar, or on their return home by the German occupier, ever hungry for latex. As for the ships in the Far East, all were seized by the Japanese with no compensation in any form (polite language calls this the 'right of angary' - stolen is the better word), and - ironically - had to be taken to Japanese ports by their French crews.

However, under Vichy Rule, and particularly under the auspices of Admiral Auphan, the Direction des Transports Maritimes started planning – somewhat in advance – for the post-war period: from these studies would come many types of ships, most of them for the vital North African link. First would come the 'tranches de melon' (melon slices), 2,500 tons with Maierform hulls, then the 'Sidi' class of cattle carriers, of which a few examples would be built by Denny post-war. Units of 5,000 deadweight would emerge as the 12 ships of a fast class with engines-aft for the North African route; another class, the 7,000 tonners, became Chargeurs Réunis' B class for the West African route. The third design, also for Chargeurs, would become particularly ubiquitous: 10,000-ton-deadweight ships that would eventually emerge as cargo ships for the Messageries Maritimes and as the passenger cargo ships of the 'Savant' class for Chargeur's Réunis and Sud Atlantique.

Yet, in 1946 the French Merchant Fleet looked much like the scuttled fleet at Toulon: leftovers from an ogre's meal. Of the magnificent Messageries Maritimes pre-war fleet, only 34 ships remained out of 80 with an average age of 26 years, whilst the cargo ships of First World War vintage were even older. Worse, this time the Empire was showing ominous signs of cracking at the edges, after the Setif revolt and the beginning of the Indo-Chinese insurgency.

Once again, the French Republic took a hand, through the person of Jules Moch, in the form of a complete reorganization of both state-run companies (Compagnie Générale Transatlantique had been all but nationalised in 1932). For Messageries Maritime, the medication would be very strong: gone was the distinction between the privatised cargo and the passenger services. Whilst public services run under stringent conditions were the primary goal, the legislator also now asked for 'value for money', with special emphasis put on the freight services, thus recognising the inroads of air travel on the passenger ship business. The old Messageries' private sector was severed from the parent company to become a separate entity deprived of ships and of its name: thus was born the Compagnie des Transports Oceaniques (CTO), handicapped by a *fifty-year* non-concurrence clause and having already sold all its shares to Chargeurs. It was condemned to operate on a round-the-world service, which was fully absorbed by Chargeurs in 1957.

Maréchal Joffre of 1933 spent the war in the Far East and the Pacific. She was handed over to the U.S.A. after Pearl Harbour, although continuing to fly the French flag for several months, which is probably when this photograph was taken. In April 1942 she was converted at San Francisco into a hospital ship, renamed *Rochambeau* under the U.S. flag and spent the war ferrying casualties from the Pacific War back to the U.S.A. Handed back to France in July 1945 under her original name she worked mainly as a troop ship and refugee carrier until taken in hand for rebuilding in 1951. *[Ian J. Farquhar collection]*

Messageries Maritimes emerged in 1948 as a newborn entity – a 'société d'économie mixte' - with a 75% state stake, and a high priority for the allocation of cargo ships, a legacy of the Indo-Chinese revolt. All this with a hopeless fleet of near derelicts: *Lieutenant St. Loubert Bie* (1911), *Maréchal Galliéni* (1912), *Yang-Tse* (1915), *Comandant Dorise* (1917), *Lieutenant de la Tour* (1917), *Sontay* (1921) and *Espérance* (1923).

Liberties and foreign built ships

The freight department was not at first over enthusiastic about the Liberty ships (these were actually leased from the French government, so the lines could not give them any major rebuilds, hence their scepticism). They were slow compared to pre-war units (which had all been modernised with Bauer-Wach exhaust turbines and were good for 14 knots), and lacked the necessary derricks to handle cargo in the vast 3,000 cubic metres of number 2 hold. Worse, the ships were deemed by their crews as virtually uninhabitable in tropical climes: the steam pipes for the winches crossing the chief officer's quarters were especially criticised. Only six were requested from the Direction des Transports Maritimes at first, but the Indo-Chinese insurgency, with its ever increasing needs, ensured that more units were eventually requisitioned, some even coming from French Line. In the end, the line ran 19 Liberties on various services until 1961, plus quite a number of chartered ships (up to 25) during France's involvement in Indo-China. These ships were used indiscriminately as troopships with their original U.S. fittings, as refugee ships to evacuate North Vietnamese to the south, and finally for repatriating the Viet-Minh to their homeland from deportation camps in New Caledonia. Besides, these ships had tremendous carrying capacities, and were used profusely on the Indian subcontinent services right until the end. When they were retroceded to the French state, they were in impeccable condition (one old master I had the privilege to meet, Commandant Forrer, told me that *Saint Nazaire* was 'almost as new' when he laid her up), having been equipped with an extra two derricks at number 2 hatch, and was very well maintained. Afterwards one, the *Beauvais*, was even used for static experiments in LNG carriage with three different experimental tank types. But Liberties, good as they were, were not quite up to the line's standards: better was needed if the Australian and New Zealand services were to be maintained. Worse, the 16-knot ship remained a challenge.

The 1915-built *Yang Tsé* was one of a number of German ships ceded to France as reparations after the First World War, having been built as *Remscheid* for Norddeutscher Lloyd. Taken back by Germany in 1940 as *Markobrunner*, she was recovered at Copenhagen in 1945, repaired and returned to Messageries Maritime, for whom she worked until 1957, to be broken up two years later. *[Ships in Focus]*

Lieutenant de la Tour was built by Kawasaki during 1917 for British account as *War Queen*. These Japanese wartime ships were typically short lived, but she survived to give the company post-war service, working until 1951. Greek owners then squeezed another three years out of her as *Cleophile Ioanna*. She is about to transit the Suez Canal: note the searchlight on her bow. *[Ian J. Farquhar collection]*

Lieutenant Saint-Loubert-Bié was another reparations ship, the former *Mannheim* of Deutsch-Australische D.G. Although well past her prime, the 1911-built steamer was sorely needed for Far East services, given the insurgency in Indo-China. A Viet Minh mine but an end to her long career in August 1950. *[Author's collection]*

Somewhat reluctantly, Messageries Maritimes eventually operated 19 Liberties, all of which had been bought by the French government.

Top: Photographed in July 1952, *Beauvais* was built at Wilmington, North Carolina as *John Lawson*. In 1960 she was converted to a liquid gas tanker to investigate the feasibility of carrying methane from Algeria. Like similar examples elsewhere, she did not trade commercially and, after use as a storage vessel, was broken up in 1967. *[Roy Fenton collection]*

Middle: The Portland, Oregon-built *George W. Campbell* became *Saint Valery-en-Caux* on acquisition by France in 1947, her name being shortened to *Saint Valery* on transfer to Messageries in 1948, but restored in 1956. Sold in 1962 to become the Lebanese-flag *Henriette*, she too was demolished in 1967. She was photographed at Sydney on 23rd July 1949. *[David Finch/ Russell Priest collection]*

Bottom: Seen in 1961, *Le Verdon* was built at Brunswick, Georgia as *Victor Herbert*. Transferred to Messageries Maritimes in 1952, she was broken up at Bremerhaven in 1963. *[J. and M. Clarkson]*

Two British-built Empire-types were bought. *Empire Rawlinson*, soon renamed *Monkay* (no offence meant - just another 1945 lost battle in northern Tonkin), was a huge but slow (14-knot) six-hatch ship with 20 derricks, and three heavy-lift derricks which proved ruinously expensive to operate with French crews on 40-hour working weeks. *Empire Gala*, soon renamed *Bir-Hakeim*, was more popular with crews, especially considering her capacity for 36 cabin-class passengers plus a possible 200 in steerage for an intended Australian service. This plan was soon crushed by Bureau Veritas, which prohibited her from carrying more than 12 on account of her lack of waterline subdivision. In this case, an 80-tons-per-day bunker consumption must also have proved somewhat expensive, even if she was and still is regarded by old timers as most elegant and comfortable.

Another unit reallocated by the Direction des Transports Maritimes rebuilding programme was *Indus*, formerly CGT's *Pérou*, taken over by Messageries Maritimes on the stocks at Burmeister & Wain's yard in Copenhagen. She was a very fine, five-hold, three-deck, 16-knot shelter-decker, with twin screws powered by Burmeister diesels. Her sole weakness resided in her patented Burmeister hatch covers which had a tendency to fold when not locked properly, and to precipitate the unwary mate or sailor down the hatch. Unlucky as she was, she still managed to reach a ripe old age in the company, not being sold until 1973, and that sale being for a single voyage to the breakers.

Fabre Line's *Pierre de Saurel* became *Anadyr* in 1953, a 7,000-ton deadweight unit of the wartime-designed B class, generally associated with Chargeurs Réunis. She proved to have inadequate carrying capacity and insufficient speed for her intended services (Chargeur's B types were all stretched in 1961 to reach 10,000 deadweight), and was more or less limited to the Indian Ocean service for her entire life. Her accommodation, with part of the crew aft, also made her unpopular because it was far below company standards.

Last, but apparently not least, came Leif Höegh's *Hoegh Clipper*, built by Howaldtswerke at Kiel, and bought in 1953 to become *Donaï*. She represented progress at its best and its worst. On the positive side, her accommodation was something of a wonder in 1954, with full

Monkay was a diesel-engined example of the British 'Fast Empire' type cargo liners. Completed at Port Glasgow in 1944 as *Empire Rawlinson*, she was taken over by Messageries Maritimes at Liverpool in January 1946. She was used mainly on Australasian routes until 1958 when sold to Greek owners who ran her as *Dimitros* until 1969. She then went to Argentinean owners, still under the Panama flag as *Tropero*, who sold her to breakers at Campana, Argentine in 1972. *[Ian J. Farquhar]*

Empire Gala was launched at Sunderland in August 1945, and quickly sold to a French government desperate to rebuild the national fleet. Whilst fitting out the turbine-driven steamer was modified, most noticeably with a round-topped funnel, and handed over in March 1946 as *Bir-Hakeim*, allocated to Messageries Maritimes' Far Eastern and Australian services. After sale in 1958, she came under Greek and later Taiwanese ownership, being broken up at Kaohsiung in 1970. The name *Empire Gala* was briefly reused for a German 'Hansa A' type, taken in prize at Kiel in 1945. *[Roy Fenton collection]*

Another post-war acquisition was CGT's twin-screw motor ship *Perou*, taken over whilst building, which became *Indus*. After use first on the service to the Indian sub-continent and Australia, and then on the route to Malaysia and Indonesia, she was sold in 1973 but broken up at Savona in 1974. *[Roy Fenton collection]*

air conditioning (albeit on a fragile and quickly outmoded principle), with most of the crew in individual cabins. She also had radar, unfortunately only accessible from a hut in the forecastle thus preventing its use, a single screw, pontoon hatch covers allowing easy watches for stevedores, and aluminium side ladders. However, she had a hopeless lack of stability which prevented her from loading any sort of deck cargo, a feature that other company ships would inherit, and an unreliable M.A.N. double-acting engine, which would prove constantly worrisome in French hands (although it did not leave any bad memories with an engineer friend – in contrast to some unfortunate Stork or Pielstick engines, which were loathed by whole generations of engineers). Ultimately, lack of stability spelt her doom, and explains her premature demise.

Rebuilding a fleet from scratch

Given the conditions, the first task was to eliminate one obvious problem: traces of German sabotage to French shipyards, which effectively prevented any serious rebuilding until early in 1948. This involved the clearing of launching ways, such as the two sabotaged 15,000-ton deadweight fleet oilers in Dunkirk which would eventually emerge as *Rhône* and *Saône* and would serve the French Navy until the late seventies. Plus, to some degree, clearing the yards of German tonnage ordered under the Hansa programme, such as the three 11,000-ton deadweight ships ordered from Penhoët, which would eventually materialize as French Line's W class, *Washington*, *Winnipeg* and *Wyoming*. Simultaneously, attention had to be given to channels, graving docks, harbours (in Le Havre alone lay 700 wrecks), which in turn would provide the shipyards with units worth reconditioning, numerous mine fields to be dealt with, and the extensive effort needed to rebuild steel works and engine factories.

Re-organisation of the companies has already been briefly mentioned. This meant that priorities now had to be set between services and owners, all seeking a share in the post-war boom, with the proviso of excluding any firm which had any dealings with the Germans. As ever in France, the state through the Direction des Transports Maritimes set all priorities. France's dire financial straits dictated that naval yards would play an equal rôle in rebuilding the French merchant marine, of which most units would be state owned

Ships acquired second-hand				
Name	Year	GRT	Builders	Subsequent history.
Monkay ex *Empire Rawlinson*	1946	9,912	Lithgows, Greenock.	1958: *Dimitrios* (Gr). 1969: *Tropero* (Pan). 1972: b/u Campana.
Bir-Hakeim ex *Empire Gala*.	1946	9,071	J.L.Thomson, Sunderland	1958: *Marionga Maris* (Gr). 1965: *Ever Lucky* (Pan). 1968: *Maritime Express* (Tw). 1970: b/u Taiwan.
Indus ex *Pérou*	1951	6,919	Burmeister & Wain, Copenhagen	1973: *Encicla* (Gr). 1973: b/u Savona.
Anadyr ex *Pierre de Saurel*	1953	4,513	Sorel (Canada)	1965: *Malagasy* (Mdgr). 1968: *Malagasy* (Lib). 1978: b/u Castellon.
Donaï ex *Hoegh Clipper*	1954	9,557	HDW, Kiel	1967: *Plate Master* (Pan). 1972: *Chieh Shun* (Chn). 1977: *Cheer Ocean* (Chn). 1978: b/u Taiwan.

One of 18 sisters ordered by the French government, the Canadian-built *Anadyr* was bought in 1953. She had been completed by Marine Industries Ltd. for Cyprien Fabre. The comparatively poor standard of her accommodation made her unpopular with French crews. *[Roy Fenton collection]*

The German-built *Donaï*, another second-hand purchase, this time from Leif Höegh and Co. of Oslo, proved something of a curate's egg - some aspects of her were good, others bad. *[Roy Fenton collection]*

Maréchal Joffre seen in post-war condition. She lost her distinctive funnels during an major rebuild in 1951 which extended her life until 1960. *[Ian J. Farquhar collection]*

and leased to private companies: freighters were thus to be built in the Brest and Lorient naval yards.

First and foremost was the need for passenger ships to carry troops and civil servants to the colonies, where control had to be re-established. This involved the delivery of *Marseillaise* in 1949, and the reconditioning of *Felix Roussel*, *Maréchal Joffre*, *Eridan* and *Champollion*. Other ships were just partially reconverted from troopers with what materials were available at the time, one (*Leconte De Lisle*) was even recovered from the Japanese, fully reconditioned after having been half-sunk in Maizuru.

Then and only then could an ambitious passenger ship building programme be started, calling for three 13,000-ton/21-knot ships for the Far East (MC class), four 10,900-ton/17-knot vessels for the Indian Ocean (MD class), and two 12,600-ton/17-knot vessels for the Pacific route (ME class). Three ships for branch services were also called for: *Polynesie* for the Australia-New Caledonia route, and *Gallieni* and *Imerina* for the Madagascar coastal service.

As for the freighters, plans had been in place at Direction des Transports Maritimes since 1942-4, and were given over to house engineers Falcoz and Janet, who had been responsible for the last of the pre-war designed mail ships, *Marseillaise*, and most of the reconditioning plans for old liners, and

most likely the MC class. Their 1951 successor, M. Sartre, was responsible for the passenger ship new buildings (i.e. the MD and ME classes), which I think explains some changes in general arrangement between *Viet-Nam* and the later units of the *La Bourdonnais* class, and the early cargo ships. Finally, in the late fifties M. Rupaud was entrusted with the rebuilding of most of the cargo ship fleet.

Post-war conditions were radically different, with inroads being made on the passenger business by air travel. The 1948 Seattle Convention also

dictated new standards for crew quarters. Speed was another issue: pre-war 10 to 12 knots was acceptable for tramps, and 14 to 15 knots for the liner trades; post-war these turned into a need for sustained, loaded speeds of up to 16 knots. Yet steam was *not* considered an option for a line which had pioneered diesel engines since 1927, with *Theophile Gautier*. In fact, steam was only used post-war on the powerful 24,000 SHP *Viet-Nam* trio of passenger ships.

One of the reasons Liberty ships had been so badly received by commercial services was the provision of

Launched at La Ciotat in 1921, *Leconte de Lisle* had a long if not always distinguished career. The turbines originally fitted did not meet specifications, and were replaced with triple-expansion machinery, delaying delivery until 1925. She was seized by the Japanese at Saigon in June 1944, and as *Teiritsu Maru* ran into a Japanese minefield in July 1945 whilst evading a U.S. air attack. The Japanese raised her in 1948 and slowly repaired her, only to hand her back to France in December 1950. She ran for Messageries between Marseilles and Madagascar for two years, and was then laid up, only to be reactivated in 1954 to ship Vietnamese refugees to the south. She was broken up in 1956. *[Roy Fenton collection]*

single 'tween decks without any special enclosed spaces, which made it difficult to adequately fill the single-level holds given the small freight consignments generally associated with the Far East trade. Clearly, three-deck ships, with silk rooms and 'soutes à valeurs' (strong rooms or locked spaces), plus limited refrigerated spaces, were needed. Finally, one important variable was the weight-to-volume ratio of freight needed on all the services, i.e. expected cargoes were supposed to have a half-ton density for each available cubic metre, whereas the Liberties had 10,800 tons for 13,000 cubic metres. Yet the two high priority services to Australia and the Far East had to be restarted quickly, along with the vital war service to Indo-China. Hence, the Empire-type purchases, the *Indus* and the *Donaï*, plus any suitable 16-knot ship on the stocks ordered by Direction des Transports Maritimes, were requisitioned for vital Messageries Maritimes services.

Such was the case for the first trio of ships effectively delivered and partially designed by Messageries Maritimes from 1948 onwards, the *Mékong*, *Meïnam* and *Peï-Ho*. As mentioned earlier, these ships had been on the drawing board since the early forties, destined originally for the Far East service of Chargeurs Réunis (before CTO had been severed from Messageries Maritimes), and intended both as general cargo carriers and as fully-fledged passenger liners for the Far East and Southern American services of Compagnie Maritime Chargeurs Réunis (CMCR).

The first two were built by Arsenal de Brest, and all others by Ateliers et Chantiers de la Loire. Thus Direction des Transports Maritimes initially ordered *Vancouver* (ostensibly for French Line, yet to CMCR plans), and *Virginie* from the Brest naval shipyard, and nine sisters from Loire Yards. At a very late stage *Vancouver* was given over to Messageries and renamed *Mékong*, whilst *Meïnam* was launched as such. The Messageries Maritimes influence is very evident when one considers the differences between the lead ship in the series and the two others. Whilst all sisters had identical bridge deck arrangements and a full twelve-passenger deck below with a large lounge aft, the first unit retained crew quarters aft, directly above the screws, and a huge elliptical, vertical funnel. The only significant Messageries Maritimes feature apparent on *Mékong*

Messageries Maritimes' first motor ship, *Theophile Gautier* was completed at Dunkirk in 1927 (above). In Vichy service, she was torpedoed by H.M. Submarine *Talisman* in the Aegean on 4th October 1941. *[Ian J. Farquhar collection]*
Third of the MC class of mail ships, the turbine-driven *Laos* (below) was delivered by La Ciotat in 1954. Sold in 1970, as the pilgrim carrier *Malaysia Raya* she was lost by fire at Port Kalang in August 1976. *[Trevor Jones/Russell Priest collection]*

The first post-war newbuildings

Name	Date	GT	Builder	Subsequent history
Mékong	1949	8,267	Arsenal de Brest	1965: *Djatimulia* (Indo). 1971: *Mulia* (Pan). 1972: b/u Shanghai.
Meïnam	1950	8,536	Arsenal de Brest	1967: *Grand Abeto* (Pan). 1970: *Tong Hwa* (Somali). 1978: b/u Korea..
Peï-Ho	1951	8,606	Ateliers et Chantiers de la Loire, St. Nazaire	12.12.1957: Wrecked Casablanca, later broken up in situ.

is a fully enclosed bridge, with covered bridge wings: a ubiquitous trade mark of the company's ships. Accommodation on the second unit was modified in a way which would set the pattern for all subsequent company units: crew on the shelter deck with engineering and catering personnel to starboard and deck departments to port, in triple or quadruple cabins, with kitchens and toilet facilities on the centre line forward of the accommodation. Officers were

one deck above, engineers to starboard and deck officers to port, the end of the superstructure being occupied by a captain's dining room to port, and an officer's mess and lounge to starboard. Streamlining, very much in vogue at the time, also materialized with prominent angled deck stanchions, an inclined and rounded superstructure front and the appearance on *Meïnam* of the famous domed funnel, which became a feature on all future cargo ships in the fleet.

First new cargo liner to be delivered to Messageries Maritimes post-war, *Mékong* had been building for CGT as *Vancouver*. In 1965 she became one of a number of the company's ships sold to Djakarta Lloyd, Indonesia. *[World Ship Society Ltd.]*

Meïnam was due to be sold to Djarkarta Lloyd with her sister *Mékong* in January 1965, but difficulties with foreign exchange meant the sale was aborted. Laid up at Hamburg, she did not find a buyer until 1967. Note her domed funnel. *[World Ship Society Ltd.]*

Peï-Ho at Sydney on 22nd June 1952. Near Casablanca on 12th December 1957, she was caught by a rogue wave which broke her steering gear and threw her on to rocks where she quickly broke her back Declared a constructive total loss just seven days later, she was sold for scrap once her general cargo had been salvaged. She had been on a voyage from Dunkirk to Kobe. *[David Finch/Russell Priest collection]*

On the negative side, the ships were unpopular because of their dangerous outfit of cargo derricks, time-consuming Mege hatch covers, and the heaviness of their fittings, which proved costly to maintain (remember the 40-hour weeks and well-paid overtime). Whilst on a par with the late-1930s NYK cargo ships, the series was somewhat underpowered with its Sulzer SD 72 engines and twin-screw arrangement, and became quickly outmoded with its inadequate cargo handling facilities and capacities (11,000 tons deadweight for 16,500 cubic metres would prove difficult to fill on the intended services).

Iraouaddy and the 'super Is'

Iraouaddy, *Gange*, and *Euphrate* were plainly blueprints for the definitive work, only lacking a powerful, single-screw engine. One interesting aspect is that they were not built by the La Ciotat shipyard, which was then working to capacity on the reconditioning of mail ships and on the post-war rebuilding for the Algerian link. The I prefix is a nickname, not exactly derogatory but almost so, often used by crews, who called them 'L'Iraouaddy', 'Li Gange' and 'L'Iphrate' (remember I is pronounced 'ee' in French). This time, Services Techniques set the specification correctly: three decks, five holds, an open shelter deck, with a capacity of 8,300 tons deadweight on a capacity of 14,000 cubic metres. Yet they retained the same inadequate, twin-screw, Sulzer SD 72 engines as their forerunners, which gave them a comfortable 16 knots at the start of their careers. All post-war diesel engines were intended to run on boiler fuel (except while manoeuvring), with heating coils in the ballasts tanks, proper centrifugation and filtration facilities. This would lead to protracted maintenance of the engines later in the ships' lives, with tell-tale soot-covered after masts. Structurally, the ships were built on the longitudinal principle, with transverse framing and double bottoms. Framing together with longitudinal joints were riveted (hence the very obvious overlapping joints on their sides), but all decks and end plates were welded. Cargo handling derricks were limited, with unstayed/linked kingposts, and only four derricks provided at numbers 2 and 4 hatches. There was one 60-ton jumbo derrick and four with a 10-ton lifting capacity. One huge improvement came with the use of Macgregor single-pull hatch covers.

Accommodation was on a par with the *Mékong* trio, with a full passenger deck terminating in a large bar/lounge at the after end, yet without the rather sumptuous provision of a forward promenade deck. Another significant rearrangement was that deck officers were relocated to starboard, and that quarters on the boat deck were similarly switched, with the radio room to port as pilot's quarters, and master's accommodation to starboard. One novelty was an inside access ladder to the bridge, shielded from the elements.

Special mention should be made of the *Euphrate*. Originally built for an intended railroad rebuilding contract in Indo-China which never materialized, numbers 2 and 3 holds were merged, thus producing an 85-foot hatch over a huge 110-foot hold. A special pentagonal mast was designed for the occasion, with oversized winches, and a 100-ton jumbo derrick arranged at the break of an enlarged forecastle. Yet, heavy as it was, the apparatus was virtually unusable, its cables being not long enough to place rolling stock at the bottom of the adjacent hold! Yet it made the ship top heavy, and prone to 'sitting on its nose'. Worse, contactors for the continuous current winches were prone to overheat and catch fire, to such an extent that seamen with fire extinguishers had to be placed in front of them in event of any heavy lifts: hopeless! And this is not forgetting that the four 10-ton derricks designed to work number 2 hold were not long enough to reach cargo in the centre of the hold, which meant protracted shifting movements.

And finally, these ships were hopelessly unstable, especially on the long-haul Pacific routes, and when having to round the Cape of Good Hope after the boiler fuel in their double bottoms had been consumed. Even so, all the series worked for twenty years on their intended services. They were plain workhorses, which their crews eventually came to like, despite their shortcomings. *Euphrate*, the lame duck among them, even gave further service as a cattle carrier until 1979.

The successful 8,300 ton F type

The initial design was reworked around a big, single-stroke Burmeister & Wain engine of the 974VTBF160 type (740 x 1,600mm and 8,300 BHP) which, with its nine cylinders, could provide enough power for a loaded, 16-knot, single-screw vessel, and was capable of sustaining over 18 knots on trials.

At first six ships were ordered, two from Ateliers et Chantiers de Provence at Port de Bouc and four,

The 'super Is'				
Name	Date	Grt	Builders	History
Iraouaddy	4.1953	6,929	Forges et Chantiers de la Méditerrannée, La Seyne.	1973: b/u Taiwan.
Gange	10.1953	6,929	Forges et Chantiers de la Méditerrannée, La Seyne.	1971: *Gange* (UMPS –Fr) 1973: b/u Taiwan.
Euphrate	8.1955	7,029	Forges et Chantiers de la Méditerrannée, La Seyne.	1973: *Elsey Fir* (Pan). 1977: *Orient Clipper* (Sey). 1973: Rebuilt Singapore as cattle carrier. 1983: b/u Shanghai.

Iraouaddy was the first of a group affectionately known as the 'super Is'. *[Fotoflite incorporating Skyfotos]*

In 1972 *Gange* was transferred to the Messageries Maritimes subsidiary Union Maritime du Pacifique Sud, but was sold for breaking up at Kaohsiung in March 1973. *[Roy Fenton collection]*

plus eventually another four, from the La Ciotat yard. Fundamentally the design was a reworked version of the *Iraouaddy*; three-deck shelter-deckers with the same provision for five holds. The vessels were built on the same principle as their forerunners, on the longitudinal system for decks and double bottoms, with transverse arrangements for the sides, yet they were fully welded this time, with

the exception of one riveted seam at the bulge joint together with another at main deck level. This time the company chose unstayed Halèn design bipod masts for cargo handling which remained the choice for all their descendants, except for the addition of a 30-ton heavy lift at number 4 hold. Given the significant space occupied by the main engine, hulls were 8.56 metres longer than their forerunners, but block coefficient was kept constant by a 70cm widening of the hulls. The best evidence of this is that deadweight remained essentially the same at around 9,000 tons (9,090 tons for the first six intended for the Far East, reduced to 8,980 tons for the last four units), a 15,000 cubic metre capacity, with the provision of 600 cubic metre tanks for latex or oil, and 150 cubic metre of refrigerated space.

Accommodation was slightly reworked, with only six passengers sharing the passenger deck; dining rooms now occupied the whole after part of the deck with the main lounge moved forward. This move, in turn, freed space for the mates' cabins (bosun, assistant bosun, writer, chief steward, carpenter, head greaser) and an improved infirmary aft. On the shelter deck, the plan remained essentially the same: deck department and messes to port, engine room and hotel staff to starboard. Four longitudinal alleyways meant that this deck could be rather noisy in harbour due to the presence of stevedores. Incredibly no provision was made for air conditioning, and the ships were so uncomfortable in warmer climes that officers usually ate at the after end of the passenger deck. Another oddity, also present on the previous ships, was the provision of private individual fridges in the officers' cabins which were sold by one officer to his replacement when changing ships. The ships still proved very popular with their crews right until their end in the seventies, and very reliable in service, proving capable of sustaining 16 knots on commercial services.

Although built to the same basic design, there were important differences amongst the series. The last four were designed for South African services and had double the refrigerated capacity, with both number 3 hold 'tween decks being refrigerated. They were also given progressively increased capacity for latex or molasses in deep tanks, or special tanks for wines in bulk. Passing from one unit to another was nightmarish for a chief officer, who had to take into account various hatch and hold dimensions for bulky items such as the ever-more common nine cubic metre container. In fact, their only deficiency was insufficient stability, especially after the closure of the Suez Canal which meant they needed refuelling in Cape Town, and yet still managed to arrive in a 'tender' condition in Marseilles.

[To be concluded]

Euphrate at Sydney: note the very long hatch over number 2 hold. Rebuilding as a cattle carrier extended her life until 1983. *[John Mathieson/Russell Priest collection]*

F-type				
Name	**Date**	**Grt/Dwt**	**Builders**	**Subsequent history**
Godavery	7.1955	6,935/9,090	Ateliers et Chantiers de Provence, Port de Bouc.	1976: *Liliane* (Gr). 1978: *Rubini F* (Pa). 1982: b/u Mumbai.
Moonie	1.1956	6,935/9,090	Ateliers et Chantiers de Provence, Port de Bouc.	1976: *Gabriele V* (Cy). 1977: *Geneva* (Cy). 1978: *Bright Tide*. 1978: b/u Shanghai.
Le Natal*	2.1956	7,050/9,090	Chantiers de La Ciotat	1976: *Trapi* (Lib). 1977: *Badile* (Pa). 1979: b/u Taiwan.
Sindh	8.1956	7,050/9,090	Chantiers de La Ciotat	1970: CTL in six-day war. 1970: *Essayons* (No). 1975: *Badr* (Saudi). 1981: b/u.
Tigre	11.1956	7,051/9,090	Chantiers de La Ciotat	1975: *Siam Rainbow* (Pa). 1983: b/u Mumbai.
Yarra	3.1957	7,050/8,980	Chantiers de La Ciotat	1977: *Nestor Glory* (Pa). 1980: b/u Taiwan.
Kouang-Si	6.1957	6,991/8,943	Chantiers de La Ciotat	1977: b/u Taiwan.
Si-Kiang	10.1957	6,997/8,980	Chantiers de La Ciotat	1978: *Takis H* (Gr). 1981: *Kaleem* (Tu). 1981: b/u Aliaga.
Yalou	1.1958	6,997/8,980	Chantiers de La Ciotat	1976: *Georgios*. 1981: b/u Mumbai.
Yang-Tse	5.1958	6,997/8,980	Chantiers de La Ciotat	1978: *Lidia H* (HK). 1978: *Lu Hai 65* (China). 1993: register closed.

The first F-type, *Godavery*, at Sydney on 28th November 1964. *[John Mathieson/ Russell Priest collection]*

The ten members of the successful F-type formed a significant part of the post-war cargo liner fleet. Here are *Moonie* (top), *Le Natal* (middle) and *Sindh* (bottom). *Sindh* was trapped in the Great Bitter Lakes along with 14 other ships in June 1967. She was abandoned to her insurers, who in 1970 sold her to Norwegian owners who renamed her *Essayons*. On her release in 1975 she was sold again, this time to Saudi Arabia, and renamed *Badr*. It seems that she was not worth renovating and she did not trade again, being broken up in 1981. *[F.R. Sherlock; J. and M. Clarkson; Roy Fenton collection]*

Three further F types: *Tigre* (top), *Yarra* (middle) and *Kouang-Si* (bottom). The last-named differed internally from her predecessors, but inspection of the photographs reveals no sign of this externally. Of the ten, only *Kouang-Si* failed to find a further buyer: after transfer to the newly-merged Compagnie Générale Maritime in March 1977, she was sold to breakers at Kaohsiung ten weeks later. *[B. Reeves; J. and M. Clarkson collection; John G. Callis]*

Completing our review of the F class (none of which were given names beginning with the letter F) are the final three, all fitted with additional refrigerated capacity for South African services: *Si-Kiang* at Cape Town (top), *Yalou* (also in South African waters, middle) and *Yang-Tse* (bottom). *Si Kiang* was the last of the ten to be sold, in 1978, and the last to survive, broken up as *Takis H* at Aliaga in 1985. [William Schell; Ian Shiffman/ Russell Priest collection; Chris Howell/Russell Priest collection]

SOUTH WEST SCENES
4. Furness at Fowey

Furness, Withy ships were frequent visitors to Fowey, and around half of the 'historic' photographs found of the port feature the group's ships loading china clay, probably for North America. Owners of the *Cotswold Range* were the Neptune Steam Navigation Co. Ltd., but she appears to wear the funnel colours of another company which Furness, Withy managed, the Chesapeake and Ohio Steamship Co. Ltd.: yellow with a white band carrying the intertwined initials 'C & O'. This company was originally a joint venture between the Chesapeake and Ohio Railroad and Furness, formed to operate cargo steamers between the United Kingdom and the railhead of the 'Chesie' at Newport News, but the

ships were later absorbed into the main Furness fleet.

The presence of *Cotswold Range* dates this photograph to between March 1912, when the steamer was delivered by the Northumberland Shipbuilding Co. Ltd., and 1914, when she was sold to A/S Den Norske Amerikalinje, Christiania to become *Trondhjemsfjord*. On 28th July 1915 she was captured, torpedoed and sunk by *U 41* between Iceland and Norway whilst on a voyage from New York to Bergen with general cargo. As neither the USA nor Norway was at war with Germany at this point, the reason for her rather deliberate sinking is unclear. The crew and four passengers were allowed time to climb into the lifeboats and were

towed by the submarine until they could be put aboard another Norwegian ship.

Just prior to the First World War, coastal sailing vessels were still common, and no fewer than eight can be seen in this delightful view of the port. Of particular interest is the small raised quarter deck steamer in the foreground. Whilst this hull layout was very common in ships built in the last decades of the nineteenth century, this one is unusual in that the white-painted structure below the bridge is particularly narrow. Her name cannot be discerned and she flies no national flag, the only clue to her identity being the yellow funnel with a darker band on which is a white letter 'M'. Is she Norwegian, perchance? *[Roy Fenton collection]*

The clipper-bowed steamer (far left) is the second *Evangeline* (2,268/1891) owned by Furness, Withy, the former *Clan Mackinnon*, acquired in 1902. She was sold to Greek owners as *Pelagos* in 1909, but after grounding off Barry in 1912 was broken up by Wards at Morecambe.

At the back is Furness, Withy's *Gloriana* (3,051/1905). Sold to Belgium

as *Remier* in 1912, she lasted until June 1945 when, as the Japanese *Kenjo Maru*, she was torpedoed by a US submarine.

The third recognisable ship is yet another Furness vessel, the 4,262gt *Powhatan*, built in 1900 as a cattle carrier – the permanent stalls on her deck can just be discerned. She also was sold in 1912, going directly to Japanese owners as *Senju Maru*, and going missing in

November 1915, probably a U-boat victim. The black funnel of *Powhatan* indicates a date after 1905 when she would lose the predominantly yellow funnel of the Chesapeake and Ohio Steam Ship Co. Ltd. on transfer to the ownership of Furness, Withy and Co. Ltd. itself. The photograph can therefore be dated to between 1905 and 1909. *[J. and M. Clarkson collection]*

The *Tabasco* (left) was well photographed at Fowey, possibly because of her picturesque if archaic bowsprit, but probably because she was a regular visitor. Completed by James Laing, Sunderland in 1895, she was registered in the ownership of the Neptune Steam Navigation Co. Ltd., her name reflecting the preferences of the original managers of the company, W. and T. W. Pinkney, also of Sunderland. Furness purchased seven of the financially-troubled Neptune company's ships, including *Tabasco*, and its Rotterdam to Baltimore liner service in 1906. The company itself became a Furness subsidiary in 1910.

Tabasco remained with Furness for longer than did many younger ships. On 26th January 1917 she was captured, torpedoed and sunk by *U 54* west north west of Ireland whilst she was on a voyage from Halifax to Liverpool with general cargo. *[Roy Fenton collection]*

'Furness liner *Oriana* loading china clay at the new electric tip' is the caption on the lower photograph. The description of 'liner' is justified, as in 1912 the 1902-built *Oriana* was transferred to the British and Argentine Steam Navigation Co. Ltd.

to work alongside the meat ships of Houlder Brothers running from South America. She had been built (by the Northumberland Shipbuilding Co. Ltd.) with a modest refrigerating capacity, which was enlarged around 1912. On transfer, Houlder Brother's funnel colours would then have replaced the plain black funnel she wore at Fowey.

The transfer may have been a stop gap to await the delivery of new ships built for the meat trade, as after less than two years *Oriana* was sold to Japan as *Java Maru*, steaming on under various ownerships until broken up in 1933. *[Roy Fenton collection]*

If Furness, Withy did have a ship naming philosophy in the early twentieth century, it is not immediately apparent, as names from northern England, the USA, ranges of hills, ones ending -iana and various others are scattered through the fleet. *Washington* of 1907 could fit into two of these categories, although initial ownership by the Chesapeake and Ohio Steamship Co. Ltd. certainly suggests that the US state or city inspired it. In 1908 she moved to straight Furness, Withy ownership, presumably adopting the plain black funnel seen here. Builders were the Furness-owned Irvine's Shipbuilding and Dry Docks Co. Ltd. at West Hartlepool.

In 1914 *Washington* was sold to Antwerp owners, first as *Ertshandel*, and by 1916 had passed to Lloyd Royal Belge S.A. as *Chilier*. Although still registered at Antwerp, she would by now be controlled by Belgians in exile in the UK, and paid the price on 22nd June 1918 when she was captured, shelled and sunk by *U 151* whilst on a ballast passage from Barry to Sandy Hook. *[Roy Fenton collection]*

Peruviana was built by Ropners in 1905 for personal ownership by Christopher Furness, but quickly passed to his British Maritime Trust Ltd., and in 1909 to Furness, Withy and Co. Ltd.

Her sale to Russian owners in 1914 as *Zhulan* saw life becoming rather more adventurous. In 1918 she was in Helsinki, 'seized by White Finns', according to one source, but also believed to have served as a hospital ship for the Russian navy and to have helped evacuate parts of Russia during the war and the Bolshevik revolution. The Finnish Government took her over, and resisted legal action by her former owners when she was arrested in Antwerp during January 1920. The new Russian government, desperate for shipping, managed to negotiate her return to their flag under a treaty which recognised an independent Finland, and she came under Soviet control in July 1922, now named *Kamo* (a photograph of her under this name appears in Bollinger's 'From the Revolution to the Cold War'). She was later transferred to Vladivostok, and was wrecked on Karaginski Island in the north Pacific on 9th December 1936. *[Roy Fenton collection]*

Cleveland Range (above) was one of three Doxford Turrets owned by Furness, Withy, and the only one bought second-hand. She was completed in 1898 as *Heathdene*, for Newcastle owners, becoming *Forest Dale* within months. The Neptune Steam Navigation Co. Ltd. acquired and renamed her in 1910, but did not retain her long, and in the great clear out of tonnage which preceded the First World War she went to Italy as *Giuseppe G.* Her fate is a little mysterious: destroyed by an explosion, cause unknown, off Cape Polonio whilst voyaging between Buenos Aires and Rio de Janeiro on 24th July 1918. *[Roy Fenton collection]*

Malvern Range (below) was built by the yard of Furness, Withy and Co. Ltd. at West Hartlepool in 1906 for the Neptune Steam Navigation Co. Ltd. based in Newcastle-upon-Tyne. In 1914 she went to Russia as *Zimorodock*, presumably part of the same deal which saw *Peruviana* also go to the St. Petersburg-based West Russian Steamship Company. For reasons not immediately apparent, *Zimorodock* was taken over by the Shipping Controller in April 1918 and given to Ellerman's Wilson Line Ltd. to manage. In April 1920 she was officially returned to her former owners, but immediately sold to Glover Brothers of London, who – perhaps not seeing a long-term future for her – did not bother to rename her. A decent wartime photograph of her in Manchester as *Zimorodock* appears in our 'British Shipping Fleets' Volume 2, page 187. Following sale to Greek owners as *Ermoupolis* in early 1928 she did not survive long, a stranding at Lobeira in Argentina during September 1931 saw her dispatched to breakers at Ferrol after refloating. *[Roy Fenton collection]*

Cynthiana (above) was built by West Hartlepool's major shipbuilder, William Gray and Co. Ltd., for what was arguably the town's most prominent ship owner, Christopher Furness who, by the time of her delivery in 1905, had become Sir Christopher. Her career followed the familiar pattern inside the Furness group of transfers, first to the British Maritime Trust Ltd. in 1906 and then to Furness, Withy and Co. Ltd. in 1909, presumably without change to her trading pattern. She was part of the 1914 sale to the West Russian Steam Ship Co. Ltd., for whom she became Egret. She was mined and sunk on 28th January 1917, five miles south west of the Inner Dowsing Light Vessel whilst carrying timber from Archangel to London. The Starke-Schell Register for 1905 speculates that the mine had been laid the previous day by the German submarine UC 26. [Terry Nelder collection]

A Fowey tug much older than those featured in 'Record' 56 tows an empty lighter past Station End (below). Unusually for Fowey, the only other vessel visible is a very small sailing craft.

FOWEY. STATION END.

Leaving Fowey in tow, *Cutty Sark* (above) is returned to Falmouth in August 1924 having been brought round from Falmouth on 3rd August to take part in the port's Royal Regatta. At the time she was being run as a training ship by Captain William Dowman who had bought the 1869-built former tea clipper from Portuguese owners as *Ferreira*. On Dowman's death she was transferred to the Thames Nautical Training College at Greenhithe, to become an auxiliary training ship to HMS *Worcester*. It was not until 1954 that she was put on display in the dry dock at Greenwich where she remains.
[Fred Kitto/J. and M. Clarkson collection]

Before 'South West Scenes' sails westwards to ports anew, the bucolic scene at Fowey below contrasts with the activity at and around the china clay tips. The two vessels below - possibly a Scandinavian three-masted schooner and a well-laden British example alongside - are a reminder that before the china clay export business began to boom in the mid-nineteenth century, Fowey was a town of shipbuilders in wood, of small ship owners, sailormen and - given the poverty of much of the south west of England - much illegal activity involving smuggling and piracy.

As a natural harbour, the River Fowey was rivalled only by Falmouth. Its exports were mainly mineral ores and building stone, plus grain and some locally-caught fish, whilst imports were merely the few necessities of life that the local population of fishermen, miners and labourers could afford.

In his study of Fowey's ships and men, 'Ships and Shipbuilders of a Westcountry Seaport: Fowey 1786-1939', Ward-Jackson cites resentment of the state for its taxes, and loathing of the established church by a largely non-conformist population, as justification for the piracy and smuggling for which Fowey was notorious. In particular, the port's strong connections with Guernsey were a cover for much of the 'trade' in goods smuggled from France. In the mid-nineteenth century, the port did share in the modest prosperity enjoyed by builders and owners of schooners, but - with modest exceptions described in the next issue - this was not translated into ownership of steam ships, and Fowey's china clay was largely moved by ships owned elsewhere.

WE BUILT A SWIMMING POOL

Andrew Bell

Post-Second World War, Blue Funnel and Glen Line are remembered as dominating the Europe to Far East trade routes, whilst Blue Funnel also had a significant presence in the UK to Australia trade. These were richly remunerative and well protected from speculative competition by the liner conference system which was at the zenith of its power. However, pre-war Blue Funnel also had an interest in the trans-Pacific trade, a result of the spree of shipping company acquisitions which took place between 1915 and 1917, and in which Blue Funnel were active players. In August 1915 Alfred Holt bought Royden's Indra Line – neighbours in Liverpool – for £750,000 giving Blue Funnel seven ships and conference rights between the East Coast of the United States and China. There was little doubt that Richard (later Sir Richard) Holt (1868-1941) recognised the potential of the Panama Canal for, in February 1915, when the waterway had been open for only six months, the *Astyanax* (1) (4,872/1906) passed through. In the 1920s this cross trade developed into a trans-Pacific one, Blue Funnel establishing a presence in Puget Sound in the Pacific North West.

Belief in the area's potential for continued growth led in 1950 to an operational arrangement with De La Rama Steamship (of the Philippines) which also involved Brostrom's Swedish East Asia Company. It was opportune that other shipping companies serving the trans-Pacific trade were losing their nerve. Citing the devaluation of the pound against the US dollar in 1949, some had withdrawn, including Silver Line-Barber, Prince Line and Moller's Lancashire Shipping Co. Ltd. Blue Funnel's own Puget Sound service was not re-established after the Second World

War: having lost half its 80-ship fleet during the war, Holt's new buildings were destined for the mainline routes as a matter of priority. However, in 1954 Blue Funnel began to contribute ships to the De La Rama Line, usually vessels that were misfits on the primary services, consisting of pre-war or wartime survivors, the newest of which was the *Telemachus* (4) (7,868) built by Caledon at Dundee in 1943.

The *Telemachus* had the distinction of being the prototype of the 28 *Anchises* class built between 1947 and 1958. She was designed by the company's in-house naval architect, Harry Flett. With feedback from her in service he had time to refine the design, the lead ship to emerge being the *Calchas* (3) (7,639/1947) and the last the *Ajax* (4) (7,974/1958). There were plenty of mistakes evident in the *Telemachus* that were corrected in the class-to-be, not least of which was the austerity finish. She had bare steel decks where timber sheathing was needed, an unfinished look to all her cabin accommodation, and a none-too-reliable Burmeister & Wain/Kincaid double-acting, eight-cylinder main engine that, carefully managed, could produce 14 knots. Twelve passengers were accommodated in five cabins on the starboard side of the promenade deck.

Ever since Lawrence D. Holt (1880-1962) started a training programme in 1917 he insisted that cadets should have a special status on the ships on which they served, and continuing a tradition of the English East India Company they were to be called midshipmen. They were to have the widest possible experience during their three- or four-year apprenticeship and even had their own department in head office at Liverpool. With around 70 ships in the fleet by

The *Telemachus* of which Andrew writes was the fourth of Holt's ships to be given the name. The third was laid down in February 1940 as a repeat of the twin-screw *Priam* (4), based largely on the Glen Line motor ships of the 1930s.

However, what should have become *Telemachus* (3) was requisitioned by the Admiralty and converted into the escort carrier HMS *Activity*. The name *Telemachus* (4) was given to her single-screw replacement, delivered in 1943.

This ship is seen here in Blue Funnel colours off Birkenhead on 27th March 1948, and still in war rig with signal mast on the bridge and no topmasts. *[John McRoberts/J. and M. Clarkson collection]*

the mid 1950s and 'middies' on almost every ship, the total number under training could be 300 – and that was before engineer cadetships were introduced. All ships built after 1957 had half decks accommodating a total of six trainees. However, the *Telemachus* had just an austere four-berth cabin on the centrecastle deck adjacent to the dining saloon. The two-berth en-suite cabins of the *Menelaus* class of 1957 were still on the drawing board in 1954. With the appointment of a new Midshipmen's Department head in 1955, came the quarterly magazine, 'The Halfdeck', from the September 1956 edition of which the following is reproduced.

From San Francisco to Manila the *Telemachus* takes 18 days, and you can usually forecast that at least 14 days will be hot, cloudless, calm and perfect. It was with this in mind that, in snow-covered New York, the members of the half deck conceived the idea of building a swimming pool to give added enjoyment to an already happy trip. The four of us had plenty of time to design the pool as we went about our jobs but first we had to receive official approval. The granting of this seemed unlikely, but still the Chief Officer gave us a hearing; he obviously thought we were mad but said 'Yes, under certain conditions'. These were:

- that the pool must be so small that it would not affect the vessel's stability,
- that no materials were to be used in its construction that were of any value to the ship,
- that it did no damage to the ship,
- that it got in no-one's way,
- that if it was ever built it must be dismantled before Manila,
- that it was built in our own time,
- and last but not least, that the Master must give his approval.

In lesser half decks these conditions might well have put an end to this unusual project, but not so with us. In San Francisco we spent lunch hours and smoke-os searching the ship's holds for spare, old hatch boards and useless dunnage.

The plan was simple. All you had to do was build a wooden box with three hatch boards at each end, with planks for the sides, and line it with canvas. Having assembled the wood we searched in vain for the canvas. Anything whole, such as a hatch tarpaulin or an awning was out of the question, but at last we found a sizeable piece of canvas that had been consigned to the paint store from whence we acquired it. There was a good deal of discussion as to the site but eventually we settled for the port side of the forward well deck.

Out through the Golden Gate and dipping into the long Pacific swell went the laden *Telemachus*. Three days out the weather burst into its tropical splendour and work on the pool began to the accompaniment of jeers, jokes and useless suggestions. On finishing the ship's work at four o'clock the midshipmen began their own. First the six hatch boards were nailed together in two tiers; these were the two ends. While two of us assembled and hammered, the others sawed the dunnage into equal lengths to form the sides. On the second day the assembly was finished and the canvas lining was tacked in, but the dawn of realization was soon clouded when the hose was turned on. In went the water but it didn't stay in; in fact the level didn't even reach six inches: water poured out through every joint where canvas met canvas. At these seams we simply tacked the canvas to the wooden sides but this was not watertight. Temporarily the half deck was baffled, and at dinner that night there was a good deal of 'We told you so!' The critics chuckled with delight, but having gone so far we were not turning back. It was one of the deck boys who had the solution. By nailing thin battens of timber along all the joins of canvas the pool became almost completely watertight. Once again the deck line hose was turned on and this time it stayed on. As

Telemachus in 1957, rerigged compared with the photograph on the previous page, but retaining her funnel which was shorter than for the succeeding A class, for which she was a prototype. This photograph was taken in the Mersey before her transfer to Glen Line. *[Ships in Focus]*

the water level rose so did our delight. However, the more water that poured into the pool the more the sides began to bulge, and the senior midshipman's prophecy concerning internal pressures came true. Hurriedly the sides were re-inforced by shores. And so there it was, full of cool clear sea water, a monument to an idea; ten feet long, eight wide and four deep.

The pool's subsequent history was all it should have been. It was patronized by all. Former critics swallowed their pride and cooled off in it; passengers used it at their own risk; the Second Electrician even used his face mask and flippers in it. The days grew hotter, the breezes became lighter and the pool drew even more customers. Why we didn't charge admission I don't know.

We had to keep a limit of six and no more in at any one time, for though the pool was tiny, you could float in it and even swim a few strokes. Water fights were the most popular game in the pool and after getting well and truly waterlogged the participants would drain out on number 2 hatch and lie, drying in the equatorial sun. The senior midshipman pioneered diving. To do this you dived off one end with outstretched arms and hit the other. All Saturday afternoon and all Sunday we spent in or around our pool and on weekdays before breakfast, before lunch and after work. The day began and ended in it. Everywhere on board drying bathing trunks were to be seen.

A slow leak in the bottom, in the interests of hygiene, ensured the pool was emptied overnight so we filled it first thing in the morning. However, as in modern airliners, the varying pressures caused fatigue in the sides and three times the forward end fell out. Once was when a steward dived into and through it; once for no apparent reason when the Mate was inspecting it, and the third time was the last time. Carefully we dismantled it a day out of Manila and stowed it away for further use, but we were transferred to the homeward bound *Bellerophon* (3) in Hong Kong, and as far as I know it lies in the starboard fore cabin to this day. This story has a footnote. Spurred on by the half deck's success with their swimming pool the three mates built a sailing dinghy.

The *Telemachus* was transferred to Glen Line as the *Monmouthshire* (3) in 1957 probably because she had 73,770 cubic feet of refrigerated space in number 3 hold. At the time Glen Line was carrying meat products westbound from Communist China to the Communist countries in Eastern Europe. She briefly became the *Glaucus* (5) in 1963 before being bareboat chartered to Swires's China Navigation Company, 1963-1968, as the *Nanchang* (3) and eventually

These photographs show the former *Telemachus* (4) as (top to bottom) *Monmouthshire* (1957-1963), *Glaucus* (1963-1964) and *Nanchang* (1964-1968) the last named off Otago whilst on charter to the China Navigation Co. Ltd. *[World Ship Society Ltd.; John McRoberts/J. and M. Clarkson collection; David Wright]*

sold for breaking up in Hong Kong in 1968. As the *Monmouthshire* I only saw her once more when she arrived in ballast at Sydney to load on Blue Funnel's service to the United Kingdom. This was in 1957 when as a National Service Sub-Lieutenant on HMAS *Cootamundra* there was no time to ship visit to see if 'our' pool was still extant. By 1960 most of the Blue Funnel ships were equipped with a swimming pool that could be erected on the centrecastle. Did we in *Telemachus* lead the way?

TELENA – A SURVIVOR FROM THE SECOND WORLD WAR

Captain Michael Pryce

A quick glance through a copy of the official Second World War Merchant Ship Losses will show listed the loss of the British tanker *Telena* to submarine gunfire on 29th May 1940. However, this is only part of her story, and she actually lasted until 1975.

The Anglo-Saxon Petroleum Co. (as Shell was then known) built a class of 12 tankers with double-acting diesel engines in 1927: *Bullmouth, Bulysses, Clam, Elax, Goldmouth, Marpessa, Patella, Pecten, Phobos, Spondilus, Telena* and *Trocas*. They were built at various shipyards in the U.K. and in the Netherlands. The only company to build both hulls and engines was Hawthorn, Leslie and Co. Ltd., which received orders for two ships and their machinery. In the Netherlands the Fijenoord yard constructed two, while Rotterdam Drydock Company and the Netherlands Shipbuilding Company built three hulls each, the engines being of Werkspoor-type. Palmers' Co. Ltd. built two hulls and these were fitted with Werkspoor engines licence-built by the North Eastern Marine Engineering Co. Ltd. The tankers' block coefficient was 0.795 and a speed of 12.25 knots was achieved on trials at a draught of 25 feet 4 inches. Their engines were of the double-acting, four-stroke, six-cylinder Werkspoor-type with Lugt-Zulver valve gear at the top, the lower valves being normal.

Telena was completed by the Nieuw Waterweg Shipbuilding Company at Schiedam, Netherlands in March 1927 (the shipyard had been purchased by Rotterdam Drydock Company in January 1925). She was of 7,406 gross, 4,279 net, and 10,029 tons deadweight, with dimensions of 440 x 59 x 32.7 feet depth. Few early movements from 'Lloyds Shipping Index' are available, but *Telena* is known to have sailed from Singapore on 24th August 1933 for Pauillac near Bordeaux.

Telena attacked

In May 1940 *Telena* was on a voyage from Tripoli in Lebanon, where at offshore mooring buoys she had loaded Iraqi crude pumped through a 560-mile pipeline from the Kirkuk oilfield. Bound for the Shell Francaise oil refinery at Pauillac with 9,368 tons of crude, she was attacked by *U 37* (Victor Oehrn) with gunfire on 29th May 1940 off Mudros, near Cape Finisterre, in position 42.25 north, 09.08 west. The evacuation of British troops from the beaches of Dunkirk was at its height at this time, so this event was somewhat overshadowed. She was one of eleven ships sunk by the same U-boat in this area between 19th May and 3rd June 1940. The first shell from the submarine hit *Telena's* galley oil tank, setting it on fire and preventing the adjacent stern gun from being used in defence. As a consequence, Anglo-Saxon had all galley oil tanks removed and coal bunkers were installed for use in the galley instead, a wise precaution, but a constant source of annoyance and delay during the war, as coal is usually in short supply at oil refineries!

Initial reports indicated that *Telena* had been sunk, with 33 survivors landed and three of the crew killed. But it was soon noted that she was still afloat, abandoned by her crew and still burning but being towed by Spanish trawlers. Listing to port she was eventually towed into Vigo, with the fire practically extinguished. Eleven of her crew were missing, including her master, with six killed. Information received by Lloyd's continues the story.

'Vigo 31st May. *Telena* heavily shelled and ablaze, found abandoned by Spanish trawlers; now anchored in Vigo Bay and seized by Spanish Authorities who will proceed to discharge cargo. No permit granted to go on board yet. Apparently all shell holes above waterline and tanks in

Note the plain funnel on *Telena*: the shell device was not added to the company's funnels until 1946. Recently, the much depleted Shell fleet reverted to the plain funnel. *[Roy Fenton collection]*

Photographed in the Mersey on 7th June 1939, *Bullmouth* had been built and engined by Hawthorn, Leslie at Hebburn, being completed in October 1927. She was torpedoed north west of Madeira on 29th October 1942 whilst on passage from Freetown to the Tyne in ballast. Her sinking, credited to both *U 409* and *U 659*, led to the loss of 50 of the 55 crew and gunners on board. *[John McRoberts/J. and M. Clarkson]*

Completed by Rotterdam Droogdok Maatschappij in March 1927, *Marpessa* (above) was to give lengthy service, running for three different Dutch constituents of Shell, and from 1958 serving under Venezuelan registry as a storage tanker on Lake Maracaibo. She returned to her building port to be broken up by Simons' Scheepssloperij N.V., arriving under tow on 17th April 1964. Note the shell device on her funnel in this post-war view. *[Fotoflite incorporating Skyfotos/J. and M. Clarkson collection]*

Pecten waits to sail from Eastham, after delivering a cargo to Shell's Stanlow Oil Refinery (right). One of two tankers of this class built by Palmer's Shipbuilding and Engineering Co. Ltd., *Pecten* was torpedoed and sunk by *U 57* on 25th Auguust 1940 whilst on a voyage from Trinidad to the Clyde with a cargo of fuel oil. Of the 57 on board 49 were lost according to 'Lloyd's War Losses'. *[Harry Stewart/J. and M. Clarkson]*

fairly good condition. Have asked to take charge of vessel and cargo on your behalf but no official permit, even to go on board, granted. Am in touch with British Consul. Apparently vessel below waterline undamaged, tanks in fairly good condition, above waterline completely destroyed by fire and deck bent.

Vigo 31st May. Starboard side apparently intact, port side four shell holes in superstructure aft and small shell hole exactly on waterline, stern making some water. Rivets out of some plating at waterline. Whole superstructure destroyed by fire, deck plating undulated same cause. Tanks apparently intact without loss of contents except little leakage through deck owing to slack rivets and list of vessel. Bow above waterline crumpled. Vessel listing heavily to port. Engine room burned out, impossible to appreciate damage yet. Under waterline not examined, but apparently undamaged. No official permit to go aboard yet granted.

Vigo 4th June. *Telena*, discharged yesterday 300 tons from port tank aft. Vessel has other holes in hull below waterline, one below pilot bridge, another more towards stern and third hole aft underneath one already reported. Two tanks are completely full of water. Vessel anchored on beach touching clean bottom at low water. Continuing discharge today another tank towards forward. Up to now our intervention impossible.

Vigo 7th June. *Telena*, three holes below waterline temporarily repaired. Authorities discharged about 800 tons in total, deposited Campsa (Soc. Anon. Compania Arrendataria del Monopolio de Petroles). Vessel now on level keel at all tides.

London 18th June. *Telena*, information from Vigo dated 7th June states; total crude oil lost estimated at about 600 tons. Vessel's condition, superstructure absolutely destroyed by fire and uninhabitable. Engine room also burned, only item remaining in regular condition main engine which could be repaired with spare parts supplied by the builders. Main deck undulated with several rivets shifted. Vessel could be towed. Should repairs be made, essential crude oil be transshipped.

London 27th August 1941. *Telena* towed from Vigo, around Cape Villano and along the coast of Northern Spain to Bilboa, where she arrived on 17th August.

Madrid 15th June 1942. The Compania Espanola de Petroleo Soc. Anon, recently purchased the British m.t. *Telena* which has been lying at Bilboa and which is now nearly repaired. The lengthy repairs were carried out by Sestao naval yard, Bilboa.

Hamburg 19th August 1942. Repairs to the m.t. *Telena* are now nearing completion and it is considered that the vessel will be in service next month. 'Hamburger Fremdenblatt'.

London 2nd October 1942. The following was broadcast from Corunna on 30th September; m.t. *Telena* will make her trials on 6 Oct, will be blessed and christened *Gerona*.

Vichy, 7th October 1942. The former British m.t. *Telena* was relaunched today under the name *Gerona*, after undergoing repairs at the naval shipyards at Bilboa, states a Bilboa dispatch to the Vichy News Agency. The vessel was bought by a Spanish petroleum company some time ago.'

Lloyd's considered her as a total loss in view of owners being paid in full under War Risks Policy and Spanish authorities claiming excessive figure for salvage.

Shell's commercial involvement with Spain had begun in July1919 when they had stationed their tanker *Strombus* (6,548/1900) at Puerto de la Cruz, near Las Palmas, as a bunkering storage tanker. She was replaced by *Volute* (4,006/1893) in April 1920, and she was in turn replaced by the purpose-built bunkering barge (with corrugated bulkheads) *Rose Shell* (2,606/1920), but the latter broke in half and sank in harbour at Las Palmas on 10th July 1921. In June 1921 bunkering using shore tanks and pipelines came

Gerona, the former *Telena*. [Roy Fenton collection]

into use. By 1925 expanding trade saw storage tanks built in Seville (Tablada), Barcelona, Valencia, Bilbao (Santurce) and Madrid (Cerro de la Plata). Two coasters were acquired for their marine business: *Magurio* (549/1919)) and *Musilla* (577/1920), used for carrying case-oil and drums. However, a Royal Decree in June 1927 declared a state monopoly over the Spanish oil industry, and it was awarded to the Compana Arrendataria del Monopolio de Petroleos S.A. (Campsa). The Spanish Civil War (1936-1939) had serious consequences for the Shell company, and their oil business virtually ceased.

Spain in the Second World War

By 1939 General Franco was indebted to Nazi Germany for US$212 million for its military and financial support during the Spanish Civil War. Spain maintained neutrality during the Second World War, yet was an important source of wolfram and other high-grade ores such as pyrites, lead, mercury, phosphates and zinc, plus foodstuffs, particularly citrus fruits, and Germany paid for all this with gold, manufactured goods and weapons. Both the U.S.A. and Britain placed a high priority on maintaining Spain's neutrality as, if Franco joined the Axis powers, British Gibraltar would inevitably be captured. To keep Franco amenable, the Allies provided Spain with large quantities of grain and petroleum. Spain's tanker fleet was kept busy throughout the war transporting oil from Venezuela to Spain. For a simple agrarian society such as Spain, this provided a significant surplus of oil over Spain's needs, and the difference was sold on to Germany. By the end of the war, Spain had paid off all its debts to Germany, and by 1945 Spain's gold reserves had reached US$110 million.

General Franco had more dealings with Germany than with Britain during the war. Conceived mid-1940, 'Operation Felix' was a German plan to invade Gibraltar, using German troops from Spain, and hopefully with military help from Spain. However, Franco feared that Britain might use its naval strength to retaliate against the Canary Islands, and was also concerned about Spain's shortage of oil and food, plus its other economic difficulties. Long discussions took place between Spain and Germany, but Franco clearly was not prepared to enter the war on the German side until Britain was virtually beaten, and made increasing demands of the Germans to excuse his inaction. Operation Felix was finally discarded in February 1941, but it would have made dealings by the British with Spain somewhat difficult during this period.

Spanish tankers had always operated in the Caribbean according to their own dictates, much to the annoyance of the Allies. The Spanish tankers *Gobeo* (3,346/1921) and *Campeche* (6,382/1934) had been observed in 1942 by two U.S. merchant ships rendezvousing with U-boats. In November 1942, *Gerona* – the former *Telena* - refused to obey the orders of an escorting aircraft to stay away from a convoy. The same tanker later attempted to purchase six tons of lubricating oil from a Venezuela port. It was considered that this shipment could only have been for U-boats and its supply was refused. The precarious neutral road that Spain trod, tending towards the Germans, undoubtedly had its genesis in the connections forged during the Spanish Civil War.

In December 1946 the United Nations issued a resolution condemning the Franco regime and recommended that the country be expelled from international organizations. This left Spain isolated, in a situation of misery and backwardness, and it was also excluded from the Marshall Plan, in which the USA assisted the rebuilding of Europe's economy. In 1959 Franco introduced the 'Stabilisation Plan', which liberalised outside trade. In November 1975, after the death of Franco, Spain began a transition to democracy within a framework of constitutional monarchy. Spain became a member of the European Community in January 1986, with full economic integration by 1992.

Gerona's subsequent career

Some subsequent recorded movements of the Spanish-flag *Gerona* (7,853 gross, 4,847 net) are listed in the table.

Sailed	From	To
2nd January 1946	Puerto La Cruz	Teneriffe
2nd May 1946	Teneriffe	Aruba
6th February 1947	Aruba	Spain
26th February 1951	Puerto La Cruz	Teneriffe
22nd April 1951	Teneriffe	Caripito
14th November 1953	Curacao	Teneriffe
26th January 1958	Teneriffe	Sidon
23rd May 1960	Teneriffe	Sidon
21st June 1961	Tripoli (Leb)	Teneriffe
7th December 1962	Las Palmas	Sidon
13th January 1962	Teneriffe	Casablanca

By 1969, *Gerona* had ceased being reported in 'Lloyd's Shipping Index', probably because she had stopped trading internationally and was used only on Spanish coastal voyages. I saw *Gerona* on 11th July 1974, when she was southbound off the Portuguese coast, north of Cape St Vincent, probably heading south from a Spanish port in the Bay of Biscay, when my ship was northbound from Huelva, Spain. *Gerona* was sold to Desguaces Cataluna S.A., Barcelona, and demolition commenced in May 1975, many years after her recorded 'loss' off Spain in 1940.

An undated view of *Gobeo* (above) *and* Campeche (right) photographed near Gibraltar on 2nd July 1944, both thought to have refuelled U-boats during 1942. *[Ships in Focus]*

BRITISH CARGO SHIPS AND THE 1940 NORWEGIAN CAMPAIGN
Part 2
John de S. Winser

HERON 2,374/1937 General Steam Navigation Co. Ltd., London
Serving as an ammunition supply issuing ship, *Heron* left Workington for Norwegian waters on 21st April with a cargo which included 400 depth charges and associated stores. Departing Scapa

Flow in the early hours of the 26th, she was escorted by the British destroyer *Grafton* and the Polish *Burza* and reached Harstad on 30th April. Despite limited facilities, during her five weeks at Harstad and in Lavang Fjord she handled many thousands of tons of

ammunition and empties, whilst being subjected to numerous bombing attacks. As part of the evacuation fleet, she left Harstad late on 4th June with Fleet Air Arm personnel and RAF survivors aboard, arriving at Scapa on the 10th and Gourock four days later.

One of General Steam's larger motor vessels, built for the trade to Italy, *Heron* was transferred to Moss Hutchinson as

Kufra in 1956, but proved unsuitable because of her small hatches, and was quickly sold. After a number of Greek

owners and names, she was broken up at Split in 1974 *[Fotoflite incorporating Skyfotos/Roy Fenton collection]*

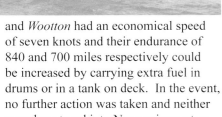
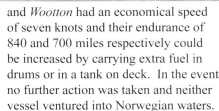

Sisters *Hilsea* (left) and *Wootton* (right) did not go to Norway but remained on the ferry service to Fishbourne until scrapped in 1961 and 1962 respectively. *[Both: World Ship Society Ltd.]*

HILSEA 149/1930 Southern Railway Company, London
On 6th May, enquiries were instigated to establish whether this Portsmouth-Isle of Wight double-ended vehicle ferry and her running mate *Wootton* would be capable of making the passage to

Norway to take part in operations. It was subsequently adjudged that they would be suitable, having sailed to the English south coast from their builders at Dumbarton, although it was admitted that both had been forced to shelter during their respective passages. *Hilsea*

and *Wootton* had an economical speed of seven knots and their endurance of 840 and 700 miles respectively could be increased by carrying extra fuel in drums or in a tank on deck. In the event, no further action was taken and neither vessel ventured into Norwegian waters.

JACINTH 650/1937 William Robertson, Glasgow

The ammunition supply issuing ship *Jacinth* left Crombie on the evening of 19th May and, escorted by the anti-submarine trawlers *King Sol* and *Loch Monteith*, arrived at Harstad on the 25th. With the evacuation of British forces from Norway already decided, the ship sailed on 29th May for Scapa Flow, where she was retained from the 3rd-29th June.

JOHN HOLT 3,815/1938 John Holt and Co. (Liverpool) Ltd., Liverpool

Allocated to Norwegian operations as a military store ship, *John Holt* was loaded with medical supplies and general cargo: she left Newport on 22nd April and Gourock three days later for Scapa Flow. Although originally intended for Namsos, the ship's destination was switched to Andalsnes but, as soon as the vessel reached Scapa on 28th April, the decision was made to withdraw British troops from that port. Her voyage was abandoned and she left Scapa on 3rd May to be back at Newport three days later.

LOCHEE 964/1937 Dundee, Perth and London Shipping Co. Ltd., Dundee

Laden with cased petrol, *Lochee* left Swansea on 9th April but, in Scapa Flow at 23:05 and again at 23:20 on the 14th, was involved in collisions resulting from the Royal Mail cargo vessel *Lombardy* dragging her anchors. Despite damage to *Lochee*'s hull, rigging and a lifeboat, she was able to continue her voyage and left Scapa on 17th April but was not received at Harstad until the morning of 3rd May. Her return voyage commenced on 8th May, with the coaster reaching Greenock on the 17th and Avonmouth on the 20th.

Jacinth (above) went on to give her Glasgow owners a remarkable total of 33 years' service [World Ship Society Ltd.]

John Holt (below) was torpedoed and sunk by *U 107* near the Canaries on 24th September 1941 whilst on a voyage from West Africa to Liverpool. [Newall Dunn collection]

Lochee sails from Leith in 1937. She was renamed *Perth* in 1948, continuing in her owner's East Coast service until 1963. After a series of Greek owners, she sank at Suez in 1979. [Graeme Somner collection]

LOCHNAGAR 1,619/1906
Aberdeen Steam Navigation Co. Ltd., Aberdeen

Originally due to sail to Namsos, *Lochnagar*'s destination was, on 19th April, switched to Andalsnes to deliver a shipment of aviation spirit. She sailed out of Aberdeen on the 21st, then left Thurso the following day, after embarking drivers. She departed Scapa Flow on the 24th and was undamaged despite a fierce aerial attack in Romsdalfjord when approaching her new destination of Molde on the 27th, and was subjected to further bombing next day off Alesund. After leaving Norwegian waters the need for engine repairs necessitated her anchoring on the 30th at Haroldswick on Unst, the northernmost island of the Shetlands, before calling at Scapa the following day and reaching Aberdeen on 2nd May.

Formerly *Woodcock* and *Lairdswood* of Burns and Laird, *Lochnagar* joined the Aberdeen fleet in 1930. She was sold in 1946, but lasted only until 1952 under the Panama flag as *Rena* and later *Bluestar* before scrapping. *[World Ship Society Ltd.]*

LOMBARDY 3,379/1921 Royal Mail Lines Ltd., London

Loaded with eight day's composite rations for the troops in Norway, *Lombardy* left Newport for Scapa Flow on 8th April and arrived there on the 14th. At 23:05 and again at 23:20 that night, she dragged anchor in a heavy squall, both times coming into contact with the coaster *Lochee*. In those collisions, *Lombardy* sustained damage to two lifeboats, three davits and one life raft: at 01:05 that same night she lost her starboard anchor and cable and, five hours later, her port anchor and cable. Doubts were expressed about the advisability of continuing the planned voyage but she nevertheless sailed out of Scapa northwards on 17th April and was accepted for cargo discharge at Harstad on the 24th. She returned to Newport via the Clyde on 11th May to prepare for a further voyage and this started from the Bristol Channel on 31st May. However, as the evacuation of British forces from northern Norway had already been ordered, *Lombardy* was held at Scapa after her 4th June arrival there and, her voyage aborted, she reached Glasgow on the 14th.

Lombardy had been built for David MacIver and Co., and was formally transferred to Royal Mail only in 1932. The grey hull in the upper photograph may indicate MacIver ownership. An account of working on board the steamer appeared in 'Record' 10. Still with Royal Mail, *Lombardy* was broken up at Hong Kong in 1959. *[Both: World Ship Society Ltd.]*

LYCAON 7,350/1913 China Mutual Steam Navigation Co. Ltd. (Alfred Holt and Co.), Liverpool

After arriving at Le Havre from Southampton on 23rd April, *Lycaon* loaded 18 guns, 12 of them Bofors, 82 vehicles and trailers and six motor cycles as part of a transfer of equipment to Norway from the British Expeditionary Force in France. On the 25th she left for the Clyde and six days later set sail for Harstad, in company with *Bellerophon*, in an 11-knot convoy escorted by the destroyers *Ilex*, *Imogen* and *Isis*. On completion of discharge *Lycaon* was urgently required in the UK to load military equipment for Iceland: she therefore left Harstad on 10th May, arrived in the Clyde on the 17th and moved up river to Glasgow two days later.

Lycaon (above) survived both world wars. Briefly renamed *Gleniffer* in 1951, she was broken up at Faslane in 1952. *[B. and A. Feilden/J. and M. Clarkson]*

Macgregor Laird was the sixth of the eight-member 'Explorer' class of motor ship. In 1953 she became the depot ship *Shell Quest* but was reconverted to a cargo ship as *Salamat in 1956*, and was broken up in 1961. *[World Ship Society Ltd.]*

MACGREGOR LAIRD 4,992/1930 Elder Dempster Lines Ltd., Liverpool

Laden with military food supplies, *Macgregor Laird* departed Newport on 8th April, and anchored at Scapa Flow on the 13th. High winds caused her to drag both anchors at 23:10 the following day, as a result of which her counter became holed in a collision with the Anglo-Saxon tanker *Conus* (8,132/1931). Thirty minutes later she was further damaged when *Clam* (7,404/1927), another Anglo-Saxon tanker, dragged along *Macgregor Laird*'s port side, twisting the Elder Dempster vessel's stem, wrecking two lifeboats and damaging another two. After a raft had been supplied as substitute and temporary repairs made to the ship's hull and damaged lifeboats, the vessel was able to proceed on 17th April and reached Harstad on the evening of the 24th. Her cargo fully discharged, she sailed on 4th May and arrived back at Newport on the 11th for permanent repairs at Cardiff to the damage to her stem and plates on both port and starboard bows.

MARGOT 4,545/1926 Walmar Steamship Co. Ltd. (Kaye, Son and Co. Ltd.), London

Switched to sail to Harstad instead of Namsos, *Margot* left Glasgow at midday on 26th April and Scapa Flow on 1st May. Carrying 110 vehicles, eight heavy anti-aircraft guns and 14 motor cycles, she reached Harstad on the evening of 6th May. In the early hours of the 9th she moved to Sorries before returning to Harstad where, after striking and damaging the pier, she dropped anchor to avert any further mishap, only to break off an anchor fluke which became wedged in a crevice. *Margot* left Harstad in a southerly direction on 11th May and between 06:30 and 16:30 on the 12th effected a landing at Mo, situated just north of the Arctic Circle. After returning to Harstad on 13th May for a 48-hour stay, the ship then sailed for Greenock loaded with the transport and guns of two light anti-aircraft batteries and the vehicles of a field ambulance unit. She arrived safely on the 22nd, despite being deprived by a dynamo fault of all electric current for the final section of the voyage. Four days later she berthed at Glasgow.

Margot survived the Norwegian campaign, but not the war. On 23rd May 1942 she was sunk by torpedoes and gunfire from *U 588* after leaving New York with cargo including military supplies for Alexandria. *[B. and A. Feilden/J. and M. Clarkson]*

MARINA 5,088/1935 The 'K' Steamship Co. Ltd. (Kaye, Son and Co. Ltd.), London

This ship was selected as replacement for *Balzac* and, having embarked stevedores to work the cargo, sailed from Gourock on 6th May and arrived at Stornoway two days later. There she took aboard the 38 vehicles and eight heavy anti-aircraft guns which were destined for Norway but had become stranded when *Balzac* sustained underwater damage. *Marina* departed Stornoway for Harstad on 13th May: she arrived on the 19th and, after discharge, left on the evening of the 22nd. Towards the end of that month she was nominated as stand-by ship and, consequently, was back at Harstad on 3rd June to assist with the evacuation. She left the following day with a cargo including 88 French guns, 10 French tanks and other vehicles, as well as two British Bofors guns and tractors and a quantity of ammunition and stores. Her return voyage was completed at Glasgow on 11th June.

Photographed on 4th September 1937, Kaye's *Marina* was as unfortunate as the same fleet's *Margot*. On 19th September 1940 she was outward bound from Glasgow for the River Plate when torpedoed and sunk by *U 48* in the North Atlantic. She was in convoy OB 213, which meant that all but two of her crew were rescued. *[John McRoberts/J. and M. Clarkson]*

META 1,575/1931 Clydesdale Shipowners Co. Ltd. (Glen and Co. Ltd.), Glasgow

The cargo assigned to this vessel consisted of cigarettes and tobacco, coal and coke, frozen meat and vegetables, as well as 7,000 rifles, 250 Bren guns, half a million rounds of small arms ammunition and dry rations for 15,000 troops. *Meta* left Leith on 5th May and arrived at Harstad during the afternoon of the 12th. After completion of discharge the vessel's return sailing, part of the way unescorted, started on 22nd May, giving her an arrival date in Glasgow of the 31st.

NAILSEA LASS 4,289/1917 Nailsea Steamship Co. Ltd. (E.R. Management Co. Ltd.), Cardiff

At Newport the vessel's 2,500-ton cargo assignment included Army rations; Royal Engineers', RAF, medical and NAAFI stores; bagged coal and coke; 15 Nissen huts; demolition explosives and anti-tank mines. Much of this cargo had originally been destined for Andalsnes aboard *Ciscar*, *Fair Head*, *John Holt* and *Thistleford*. Departing the Bristol Channel on 20th May, *Nailsea Lass* was due to reach northern Norway on 6th June but the decision to withdraw all British forces overtook the requirement for her cargo: consequently, she was held at Stornoway from 30th May until being redirected to the Clyde where she arrived on 14th June.

NARVA 1,575/1937 Scottish Navigation Co. Ltd. (Glen and Co. Ltd.), Glasgow

On collier duty, *Narva* left Aberdeen on 2nd May and Scapa Flow the following day for Harstad. There she sustained slight damage on 16th May from the sloop *Fleetwood* coming alongside and, three days later, by bomb splinters during an evening air raid. Her assignment completed, she left Norwegian waters on 22nd May and arrived at Glasgow on the 31st.

NGAKOA 507/38 W.A. Wilson, Southampton

As an ammunition supply issuing ship *Ngakoa* left Crombie on 26th May and Lyness four days later, sailing in the company of *Arbroath* and *Yewmount*. *Ngakoa* arrived at Tromso on 4th June and stayed until the 7th, following which she put into Lyness in Orkney early on the 14th.

Meta, seen both above and below at Preston, had a satisfactory post-war career for a steamer, giving Glen and Company 25 years' service, latterly as part of the Everard fleet. In 1962 *Meta* was sold to an Oslo-based cement company and converted to a storage barge. *[Both: World Ship Society Ltd.]*

The Dutch-built *Ngakoa* survived the war and had a long career in London ownership as *Thomas M* and with various Greek operators. *[Roy Fenton collection]*

PEMBROKE COAST 625/1936 Coast Lines Ltd., Liverpool

On what proved to be her final voyage, *Pembroke Coast* left Avonmouth on 8th May and the Clyde on the 12th, loaded with a reserve supply of 700 tons of cased aviation and vehicle fuel. She arrived at Harstad at 07:00 on 19th May and was still fully loaded next day when German bombs set fire to the adjoining oil berth and the blaze spread so rapidly it engulfed *Pembroke Coast*. Although later beached, she was in a derelict condition and was therefore sunk by the cruiser *Aurora* at 11:30 on 21st May, her crew being repatriated aboard *Dunluce Castle* (8,131/1904).

PIZARRO 1,367/1923 MacAndrews and Co. Ltd., London

This vessel left Avonmouth on 22nd April loaded with cased petrol for Norway. On passage from the Clyde to Andalsnes on 28th April, she was involved in collision with the French coaster *Paul Emile Javary* (2,471/1926), at position 58.12 north, 5.20 west, approximately 16 miles east north east of Stornoway. Extensively damaged on her port side aft and badly holed in number 3, that same day *Pizarro* was beached inside Stornoway harbour where she settled by the stern. Although refloated on 10th May, she had to be beached again and on 21st May temporarily broke away from her moorings. Her cargo was discharged overside to *British Coast* (889/1934), prior to *Pizarro*'s departure from Stornoway on 31st May. She arrived in Glasgow on 3rd June.

REDCAR 1,475/1920 P&O Steam Navigation Company, London

With a cargo including 10,000 rounds of 3·7-inch anti-aircraft ammunition and 31 tons of anti-tank mines, as well as Fleet Air Arm stores, bombs and ammunition for the aircraft being ferried to Norway aboard the carrier *Glorious*, *Redcar* left Leith on 12th May. She was due to join the main convoy from the Clyde the following day but missed the rendezvous as a result of her speed being restricted to seven knots by poor quality coal, which also left her short of fuel on arrival at Harstad on 22nd May. After the British decision to evacuate northern Norway, *Redcar*'s cargo on leaving Harstad on 31st May consisted of blankets, rifles, tents, heavy anti-aircraft ordnance and miscellaneous Army and RAF stores. She was detained at Scapa Flow from 7th to 15th June before finally arriving at Glasgow's Rothesay Dock on the 17th.

Seen in the Mersey pre-war, the unfortunate motor ship *Pembroke Coast* was not to survive the Norwegian campaign. *[Basil Feilden/J. and M. Clarkson]*

Pizarro was sunk by the Italian submarine *Dandolo* on 31st January 1941 whilst on a voyage from London to Seville with general cargo. *[Newall Dunn collection]*

Almost unique amongst P&O's fleet of cargo and passenger liners was the East Coast collier *Redcar*, built by the Goole Shipbuilding Co. Ltd. in 1920. After sale in 1946 she was briefly renamed *Greensea* by Southampton owners, then became the Danish *Arnaa* and the Finnish *Katrina*. Breakers at Dover demolished her in 1954. *[J. and M. Clarkson]*

RONAN 1,489/1938 G. Gibson and Co. Ltd., Leith

On 15th April *Ronan* left Swansea with 1,440 tons of cased vehicle fuel, 83 tons of aviation spirit suitable for flying boats and 140 tons of lubricants. Three days later she sailed from Greenock and, after a call at Longhope, Orkney on the 20th April, reached Namsos at 11:50 on the 23rd. There the order was given that as much petrol as could be landed in 15½ hours should be put ashore as the ship, escorted by units of the 12th Anti-Submarine Group, was required to leave at 03:20 the following day for Skjelfjord. From there, with the same escort, she arrived in Romsdalsfjord on 27th April, close to where an RAF Gladiator squadron was operating from the frozen lake. The following day *Ronan* left for Scapa Flow, before finally arriving back at Swansea on 6th May.

Ronan was released from service as a cased petrol carrier in June 1945, and resumed trading for Gibson Line. They kept the motor ship until 1963, when she went into the almost-inevitable Greek ownership, first as *Anna-Maria* and later as *San Antonios*. In July 1967 she foundered in the Gulf of Guinea on a voyage from Nigeria to Greece. *[J. and M. Clarkson]*

RUTLAND 1,437/1935 Currie Line Ltd., Leith

The store ship *Rutland* left Glasgow on 11th May with seven heavy anti-aircraft guns and various vehicles, together with airport preparation equipment including a crane with a 30-foot boom. She arrived at Harstad on 22nd May and at 15:00 on the 26th sustained splinter damage to her hull and superstructure as a result of bomb explosions 30 feet from her port bow. This did not prevent her from loading a homeward cargo of 10 RAF vehicles, motor cycles, hospital and other equipment. She left Harstad on 28th May, escorted by the trawlers *Angle* and *Indian Prince*, and was held at Scapa Flow between the 2nd and 12th June, prior to reaching the Clyde on the 14th.

Rutland was not to survive long after returning from Norway, going missing with all hands on a voyage from Georgetown to Larne with bauxite after dropping out of her convoy on 22nd October 1940. She is known to have been torpedoed in the Western Approaches by *U 124* on 31st October 1940. *[Newall Dunn collection]*

SPANKER 1,875/1917 Witherington and Everett, Newcastle

Departing Glasgow on 17th April and serving as a collier, *Spanker* arrived at Scapa Flow two days later, then set sail for Andalsnes on the 23rd, the voyage being punctuated by a U-boat report which prompted a depth charge attack by the convoy escorts. On entering the fjord, the convoy was subjected to continuous attacks by aircraft which had already heavily bombed Andalsnes prior to the ship's arrival on 27th April. Without unloading, *Spanker* returned to the open sea and, despite further air attacks the following day, reached Scapa Flow unharmed on 1st May. The ship put into Kirkwall on the 19th, before leaving on 4th June for Methil where she arrived next day.

Spanker was photographed on 14th December 1931 in the distinctive funnel markings of Witherington and Everett, who sold her to another Newcastle owner in 1944. Renamed *Hillsider* in 1947, in 1951 Monroe Brothers of Liverpool gave her the name *Kylefirth* for work mainly on the Irish Sea. In 1956 she went to Lebanese owners as *Fatina*, who sold her to Greek breakers in 1959. *[Ships in Focus]*

THESEUS 6,527/1908 Ocean Steamship Co. Ltd. (Alfred Holt and Co.), Liverpool

Described in the military files as a horse ship, *Theseus* left Birkenhead on 27th May and Gourock anchorage on the 29th in ballast for Norway, sailing unescorted at 10 knots. She reached Harstad on 4th June and, available as part of the final evacuation fleet, sailed at 22:00 on the 7th. After transferring a crew member to the hospital ship *Vasna* (4,820/1917) at Scapa Flow on the 14th, she was back in Gourock anchorage on the 17th.

THISTLEFORD 4,781/1928 Albyn Line Ltd. (Allan, Black and Co.), Sunderland

Loaded with general cargo destined for Norway, *Thistleford* left Newport on 15th April and the Clyde for Scapa Flow on the 25th. She had been due to reach Andalsnes on the 29th but the order to evacuate that port had already been issued, so, after waiting at Scapa from 28th April-3rd May, she was directed back to Newport where she arrived on 6th May.

WOOTTON 149/1928 Southern Railway Company, London

See *Hilsea* above.

YEWMOUNT 859/1939 J. Stewart and Co. Shipping Ltd., Glasgow

After loading cased petrol, the vessel left Gourock on 28th May with HMS *Antelope* as escort and, in the company from Scapa of *Arbroath* and *Ngakoa*, arrived at Tromso on 4th June. With the evacuation from northern Norway already in progress, she was no longer required and consequently sailed again on the 7th with her entire cargo still on board. After calling at the Clyde on 19th June, *Yewmount* arrived at Llanelly the following day.

Theseus is seen in Birkenhead's Alfred Dock with a Perseus-class sister to starboard. She was sold for breaking up at Preston in 1947. *[B. and A. Feilden/J. and M. Clarkson]*

Photographed on 24th August 1949, *Thistleford* was sold in 1950 to become the Greek *Archon Michael*. Her career ended in December 1962 when she dragged her anchor and stranded in the Gulf of Suez. *[John McRoberts/J. and M. Clarkson]*

The motor ship *Yewmount,* seen at Jersey, was to have a notable post-war career. In 1947 her owners sold her to part of the Coast Lines group trading mainly to the Channel Islands, and she became *Saxon Queen*. Transferred to Liverpool in 1959 as part of the Link Line Irish Sea container service, she took the name *Lurcher*. In January 1961 she collided with the Greek *Stamatios G. Embiricos* (8,878/1956) in the Mersey and sank. Refloated, she mouldered in Morpeth Dock, Birkenhead until sent to Preston for breaking up in 1964.

RECORD REVIEW

CROSSING THE BAR: AN ORAL HISTORY OF THE BRITISH SHIPBUILDING, SHIP REPAIRING AND MARINE ENGINE BUILDING INDUSTRIES IN THE AGE OF DECLINE 1956-1990
Research in Maritime History No.51
Edited by Anthony Slaven and Hugh Murphy
Softback 23 x 15 cms of 268 pages.
Published by the International Maritime Economic History Association, St. John's, Newfoundland at US$30.
Available from Ships in Focus Publications at £18.00 plus post and packing;£2.00 U.K. or £4.50 elsewhere.

Do not be put off by its less-than-snappy title: this is a book to be read by everyone seriously interested in why the once-dominant British shipbuilding industry sank almost without trace. It consists of edited transcriptions of 60 interviews with key figures associated with ship and marine engine building and repairing. The testimonies of yard managers, ship designers, engineers, trade unionists, politicians and civil servants provide often surprisingly frank insights into the many factors that doomed these industries.

Naturally, most managers interviewed emphasise the damaging role of unions, and especially demarcation issues. But they also – with some benefit of hindsight – mostly admit that management itself failed, not only in limiting the power of the unions, but also in not improving working, management and marketing practices or investing in new machinery. There is also general agreement that educational standards were too low throughout the industry. All too often middle and senior management had risen up the ranks with no management training, no experience outside the industry, and without a university education. Those visiting yards in Japan are struck by the contrast with the UK at all levels within the workforce and management. Although some managers cite 'unfair' competition from the Far East and Europe, there is little in the way of justification for this view, and some commentators believe that the Japanese, in particular, were simply more productive, better trained and better organised.

There is also much here on the efforts by successive British governments to investigate the industry and to take steps to remedy its many problems. With their concern about employment issues, Labour governments tend to come out better than Conservative ones, especially the Thatcher government which is widely blamed for killing off A&P, the most successful British builder. But all governments are seen to lack a clear overall strategy for maritime industries, an approach which helped yards in the Far East to prosper at the expense of those in Britain.

The interviews were conducted in 1991 and 1992 on the basis of a structured questionnaire, mainly by Anthony Slaven and Philip Taylor of the Centre for Business History at Glasgow University. They involved personnel in merchant and warship building yards right around the UK, with Scottish and north eastern English yards predominating, but also including managers from the nationalised British Shipbuilding plc, plus civil servants and politicians concerned with the industry. Trade unionists are under represented, giving just three of the 60 interviews. The transcripts of the interviews, averaging 22 pages, were edited by Hugh Murphy, resulting in an average of just under three printed pages for each. They are very readable although – disappointingly for an academic publisher – there are numerous typos, including one on the cover. There is a seven-page conclusion, which aims to put the interviews into a coherent historical context and a lengthy and very valuable bibliography of publications on the British shipbuilding industry.

The value of this book lies in the breadth of opinions expressed. As the closing paragraph puts it, readers will come to their own conclusions about the reasons for the demise of shipbuilding and related industries in Britain. Most will decide it was due to a multiplicity of factors. These include a well-organised work force whose restrictive practices reflected a history of insecurity in employment; middle management with insufficient skills and authority; higher management with too much power and not enough imagination; plus ministers and civil servants unable or unwilling to devise or implement a strategy for the industry other than baling out its losses. Sadly, no one group emerges with much credit for their part in allowing a once proud industry to collapse utterly.

Roy Fenton

PUTTING THE RECORD STRAIGHT

Letters, additions, amendments and photographs relating to features in any issues of 'Record' are welcomed (and one from 44 issues back is included here). Note that comments on multi-part articles are consolidated and included in the issue of 'Record' following the final part. Senders of e-mails are asked to provide their postal address. Letters may be lightly edited.

Saint Line to South Africa
I hate to contradict someone who was there, but I think John Goble's statement on page 174 in 'Record' 55 that *St Jessica* 'would have been carrying a cargo of manganese ore from Takoradi to Burntisland' is not correct. He says that manganese ore would be used in the steel industry and battery manufacturers but neither of those industries existed within many miles of Burntisland. What did exist at that port was the British Aluminium Company which imported several cargoes of bauxite each month, invariably from Takoradi, and I feel sure it was that ore that was being transported on the *St Jessica*. British Aluminium had established itself at Burntisland during the First World War and bauxite accounted for almost all the imported cargo at the port; by the 1930s Takoradi had become the sole port of origin. A Liberty was about the maximum the entrance lock could handle and in the 1950s a variety of tramps (some quite elderly) arrived with bauxite. In the late 1950s the Swiss-based Italian owner Sebastiano Tuillier took on the entire contract and a variety of his ships served the port for the next dozen years. Thereafter, larger bulk carriers (usually from the Norwegian owner Klaveness) anchored offshore and self-discharged into specially adapted dumb barges (the size of an East Coast collier) which were towed into the

dock. The Burntisland production facility was modernised in the 1970s but other places were able to produce aluminium on a bigger and better scale and the throughput gradually dwindled until it ceased altogether around 25 years ago, since when Burntisland has handled only a small number of coasters each year on other trades.

COLIN MENZIES, 17 Bickenhall Mansions, London W1U 6BP

French Bounty ship photographer

My late grandfather, William Arthur Wilson (1878-1957), was an avid photographer of activity on the Derwent River in Hobart and took many photos of French Bounty Ships when they called. Two of the photos in part one of John Naylon's article are his work, the *General Faidherebe* (departing Hobart) which is on page 106 of 'Record' 54 and the *Rochambeau* (also departing Hobart) on page 107 of the same issue; the originals of both photos are still held by the descendants of William A. Wilson although the negatives I believe were sold off by my grandfather well before he died and their whereabouts are unknown.

I have attached a copy of the photo of the *Duguay Truin* at the start of a race from Hobart to San Francisco with the *Anne De Bretagne* on the left, further down the Derwent River, as she had started 10 minutes before the *Duguay Truin*. By reference to the land visible on either side of the photo the race was started quite close to Sullivans Cove and the Port of Hobart and, with no breeze to carry them out of the Derwent River into Storm Bay, the crew appear to be more interested in watching William Arthur Wilson take this photograph from his dinghy.

WILLIAM BURTON, 2 Gunyah Street, Bellerive, Hobart, Tasmania, Australia 7018

[Does anyone know the whereabouts of William Arthur Wilson's negatives? Ed.]

Passages

Interested to note the *Trocas* ('Record' 55, pages 150 and 155) is fitted with a pair of hawse pipes aft although no anchors are carried in the photos. It would be interesting to know the intention behind this uncommon fitting. A four-point mooring would be a most uncommon and difficult evolution with a single-screw merchant ship unless assisted by tugs.

I thoroughly enjoyed the article on the French 'bounty' ships. I was particularly intrigued by the 66-day run by the *Ernest Legouve* from Liverpool to Hobart in 1905; this record is also noted in 'The Bounty Ships of France' by Villiers and Picard. However, the 'Examiner' (Launceston) of 4th August 1905 gives the passage as 77 days, an excellent passage nonetheless. The year 1905 was one of good passages, at much the same time (July to August):

The *Ernest Reyer* arrived at Newcastle, New South Wales from Cherbourg in 80 days in ballast.
The British *Loch Garry* arrived at Adelaide in 75 days from Greenock.
The British *Edenmore* (ex *Edenballymore*) arrived at Sydney in 75 days from London.
The British *Cambrian Princess* (ex *Manydown*) arrived at Melbourne in 80 days from New York.

The 'Sydney Morning Herald' of 28th July 1905 notes the French ship *General de Sonis* arriving from Cape Town in ballast and that she had not carried a cargo for 13 months, having sailed out to San Francisco - Australia - South Africa and back to Australia, but all these miles earned bounty.

Glancing through some earlier issues at old photos the thought occurred – 'what's missing?' Stern lights. Side lights for steamships were introduced in 1848 but it was a century later, at the 1948 Safety of Life at Sea Conference, that stern lights finally became mandatory, though to some degree they had been displayed by many ships for several

Duguay Truin leaving Hobart for San Francisco on 13th July 1909. *[William A. Wilson]*

48

decades. During the mid-1970s I was towing and about that time the additional orange stern light for tugs came into force.

You mention the smack *Sirdar*, page 189, and going to sea in small vessels. I suspect most of the still extant biographies are from the last couple of decades of sail, in iron or steel ships, almost inevitably sailing to Australia and thence to North or South America which provides a confining impression. Up to about 1885 vessels of all rigs and sizes were still going worldwide.

Among my records is the ketch *Windsor*, O.N. 51276, 58 registered tons, built 1865. During the early 1870s she traded as far afield as St. Petersburg, Russia and south to Larache, Morocco. Apart from the winter months she mainly loaded fishy products in the north of Scotland for Baltic ports. She went missing in 1902 with a cargo of spuds from Montrose to Portsmouth.

The three-masted schooner *Enfield*, O.N. 44982, 169 registered tons, built 1862, sailed regularly to Madagascar and Zanzibar until wrecked at the latter in 1868.

The small barque *Gift*, O.N. 62602, 297 gross tons, built 1870, got around too. Between December 1874 and March 1879 the *Gift* sailed as follows. Cardiff - Montevideo (Uruguay) - Callao (Peru) - Pabellon de Pica - Otago (N.Z.) - Galle (Sri Lanka) - Cochin (India) - Rangoon (Burma) - Cochin - Colombo (Sri Lanka) - London (U.K.) - East London (South Africa) - Port Louis (Mauritius) - Liverpool (U.K.) - Cardiff (U.K.) - Fernando Po (West Africa) - Bonny River (Nigeria) - Plymouth (for orders) - Havre (France).
CAPTAIN J.M. ANDERSON, 523 Louise Road, Ladysmith, B.C., Canada V9G 1W7

Robertson miscellania

In the Ships in Focus publication 'William Robertson and the Gem Line', the authors queried why the Olivine *of 1902 and* Brilliant *of 1901 had yellow funnels rather than Robertson's customary plain black. Dave Hocquard provides the answer.* The enclosed photo, copied from our local newspaper, shows what I believe to be *Olivine* (634/1902) turning in St. Helier Harbour soon after entering service.

Olivine of 1902 with the yellow funnel of the London and South Western Railway. Kevin Le Scelleur's excellent 'Channel Islands' Railway Steamers' has several photographs of LSWR ships with a buff funnel. *[Dave Hocquard]*

The London and South Western Railway and later the Southern Railway chartered Robertson's coastal steamers right until 1948, the last ones I remember being *Fluor* (914/1925) and *Corundum* (929/1925). Between the wars the Southern Railway chartered *Onyx* (592/1910), *Essonite* (642/1921), *Hematite* (722/1903) and others but they kept their all-black funnels.
DAVE HOCQUARD, Le Cotil des Pelles, Petit Port, St. Brelade, Jersey JE3 8HH
A factoid about Robertson's motor vessel Tourmaline *of 1963 reported in 'Ships Monthly' several years ago, was that her bridge windows were 'recycled', having been originally fitted in HMS* Vanguard, *whose demolition began at Faslane in 1961. Apparently, when removed one of the window frames was found to be stamped with the battleship's name. Ed.*

Trawlers at Aberdeen

John Clarkson's 'Steam Trawlers at Aberdeen' complemented my piece neatly. As a matter of interest, I also photographed the Grimsby trawler *Vanessa* at Aberdeen in May 1974, although my efforts were rather unsatisfactory quayside shots. The *Vanessa* was homeward bound from Iceland when she developed engine trouble and was towed to Aberdeen by another Grimsby trawler, the *Lord Jellicoe*. The *Vanessa* landed her catch over two days at Aberdeen and it sold for a total of £12,294.

The Polish steam trawlers of the Gdynia-based Dalmor fishing enterprise were a familiar sight at Aberdeen at that time. They were under contract to Claben, an Aberdeen fish-processing firm, to supply its factory during a protracted shortage of home-caught fish.
PETER MYERS, 68 Westbank Park, Old Meldrum, Inverurie, Aberdeenshire AB51 0DG

Anchor balls

I especially enjoyed Ian Wilson's contribution to issue 56: a little gem of social history with a quiet reminder of the troubled political history of the province. More in that vein in future issues, please.

That picture did not earn a thousand words but the consistently high reproduction values of 'Record' mean that many illustrations have a little story that rewards a careful look. A case in point is the picture of the *Edenbank* on page 234 of 'Record' 56. There she is, fully laden, on her way up to Risdon (a place where I spent my last Christmas away from home back in 1985) with the anchor ball swinging happily from the forestay. It is an oversight that I have committed myself in the past and on this occasion its presence seems invisible both to the mate and chippy, busy admiring the view, and to the bridge.

Much more punctilious are the forecastle crowd on the *Southbank* on the opposite page. They have hoisted the anchor ball although the dangling head ropes and the churning propeller both suggest that the anchor is being used only temporarily to snub the bow in a manoeuvre prior to berthing. Every picture can tell a story if the clues are there!
JOHN GOBLE, 55 Shanklin Road, Southampton SO15 7RG

Brunshausen reefer

Further to Tony Breach's letter in 'Record' 55, I have port side negatives of the three reefers in question, *Brunsbüttel*, *Brunsdeich* and *Brunskoog*. The arrangement of port side

bridge deck ports on none of these matches Chris Gee's photo of the *Frigo*. The *Brunsbüttel* has ports as singles, a group of three together and a group of four together. The other two have the ports largely arranged as singles.
BILL SCHELL, 334 South Franklin Street, Holbrook, MA 02343, USA

Gibraltar oil hulks
Michael Pryce's account of the Shell Gibraltar oil hulks fills a gap on a little known aspect of the tanker business. I can add some further details from British shipbuilders' records.

Although *Black Dragon* was laid down in June 1914, she was not launched until 27th June 1918, evidently deferred by more urgent First World War work.

Fionashell had indeed Vickers-designed engines, but they were largely built by Petters of Ipswich, taken over by Vickers about 1917. Thirteen diesels were ordered at the end of 1916 for Russian submarines, Vickers' contracts 514-526, and were sold to Anglo-Saxon Petroleum after the revolution.

Trigonia was launched as *Olympia* on 23rd October 1915, with trials on 22nd June 1916. Her Vickers' engines developed 2,500 BHP. Price when completed as *Santa Margharita* was £210,000.

Kennerleya. The apparent anomaly of a 1941-built tanker having a main engine built by Palmers which closed in 1933 is explained by the fact that her triple-expansion engine was originally fitted in *British Inventor* in 1926, which was mined on 12th June 1940, and her after part salvaged. The main engine was removed and fitted in *Empire Granite* at Furness, saving £28,000 in a final total building price of £235,000.

Nuttallia arrived at Faslane 18th October 1960 to be broken up under BISCO auspices by Shipbreaking Industries Ltd.

Trocas. Her damaged main diesel engine was replaced by a newly-built Werkspoor (Hawthorn, Leslie contract 4002) installed at Smiths Dock, North Shields on 31st October 1944.
IAN BUXTON, 12 Grand Parade, Tynemouth, Tyne and Wear, NE30 4JS

As ever, I enjoyed reading the new issue of Ships in Focus 'Record'. This time I found Captain Michael Pryce's article on Shell's Gibraltar oil hulks particularly enjoyable. It brought back memories of the view from the window of my parent's house half way up the rock. Those oil hulks were an obvious feature as one looked out to the North West. However, I had more close-up views when I accompanied my father as he supplied the ships moored alongside the hulks whilst taking on fuel.

There are excellent views of *Trocas* and *Ficus* in the 1958 film 'The Silent Enemy'. However, their appearances are brief views as the camera panned past them. Nevertheless, the mast and position of the funnel are very clear.

I believe one of the tankers supplying Avtur was the *Batissa* which ran out of Port de Bouc, the loading port for the Berre refinery. She put in to Gibraltar on 20th February 1957 and possibly early March 1958.
Two hulks omitted from the list were:

1. Norrisia (Harland and Wolff Ltd., Belfast, 8,246/1944) which is noted by Mitchell and Saywer in 'The Empire Ships' 2nd edition as being a hulk at Gibraltar from 1958 to 1960 when she was towed to La Spezia for breaking up.

2. San Melito (Palmers' Shipbuilding and Iron Co. Ltd., Jarrow, 10,160/1914) which http://wwwtynebuiltships.co.uk notes as belonging to the Shell Company of Gibraltar from 1953 until she went on to be broken up at Faslane in 1954.
BARRY AZZOPARDI, 5 Grange Avenue, Beeston, Nottingham NG91GJ

Even for a tanker, *Norrisia* had a relatively short active career: completed at Belfast in March 1944, she was reduced to a storage hulk by 1958. The coaster alongside her with a deck cargo of motor vehicles has yet to be identified. *[J. and M. Clarkson collection]*

San Melito was one of the supertankers of her day, completed for Eagle Oil and Shipping Co. Ltd. by Palmers' in November 1914. Although attacked by German submarines in 1915 and again in 1917, she survived both world wars, although her role in the second conflict is not known (she is not mentioned in the relevant chapter of 'Eagle Fleet', and perhaps was used for storage purposes). In 1946 *San Melito* was bought by Anglo-Saxon Petroleum Co. Ltd. for use as a depot ship, first at Shanghai, later at Singapore and finally at Gibraltar. *[C. Downs/J. and M. Clarkson collection]*

Crescent corrections

On page 122 of *Crescent Shipping* the entry for *Bold Knight* (BK 10) states: *13.6.1979:* Sold to Tyne Tees Waste Disposals Ltd., Middlesbrough, renamed CHERRY B (changes not registered).

Photographs taken locally by myself and others show that, in fact, she continued to operate on the Tees for some time while retaining the name *Bold Knight* (my own latest photo with this name being late January 1982). It is understandable that her renaming, being unregistered, was misprinted as *Cherry B.* Her new name was actually *Cherrybee* which she carried from at least August 1983. I attach my own photo showing her under this name taken on the Tees on 3rd June 1984.

Cherrybee, 3rd June 1984.   *[Ron Mapplebeck]*

Page 129, BERMONDSEY (BK 32). According to my personal records she carried the unregistered name of *Cherrymarine* from 1974 until broken up in 1979. It is believed the ownership style was Cherry Marine Ltd., although the principal owner seemed to use a variety of identities for his several activities. Paul Hood from Blyth says he has her recorded as *Cherry Marine*, owned by Tees Partners, when arriving there to be broken up. However, I believe the rendering was as one word.

I have a photo of her on the Tees on 30th August 1977 (seemingly showing only the *Cherry* part of her name). RON MAPPLEBECK, 8 St Margarets Grove, Acklam, Middlesbrough TS5 7SB.

Amelia

My eye was immediately caught by Graeme Somner's photograph of the *Amelia* on Page 195 ('Record' 56). Although I had started to take an interest in shipping on the Forth by 1955, when she was broken up on the north bank of the river at Charlestown, I don't recall ever seeing her – nor was I ever even aware of her existence. Coopers of Kirkwall occasionally sent ships into Forth ports, but not that often: sometimes they did the occasional trip for the North Company while one of their ships was having her annual dry docking. I can pinpoint exactly where the photograph was taken, which was at the top end of the Outer Harbour at Leith viewed from the east bank of the Water of Leith. The ship seems to be near-stationary. Immediately above her stem is the entrance to the Victoria Dock, whose cranes are visible at the left-hand edge of the photograph. That dock was still in regular use in the 1950s: its south side was the regular discharging point for coasters bringing bagged cement from the Thames and there were usually two ships discharging that cargo on any given day. The north side was less heavily used but still saw regular visits by the smaller cargo ships of the North of Scotland, Orkney and Shetland Company. About 70 yards straight ahead of the ship was the big swing bridge giving access to the Inner Harbour. In those days, the bridge was still used, although not that frequently. On the east bank was a berth still used for cargo-handling by the North Company's small *St. Clement*, above which there was room for a couple of ships to lay up. An elderly 1,500 gross steamer called the *Kaupo* was there for quite a long time - I

think her owners had a Latvian or Estonian background and I suspect they may have gone bankrupt as she lay there for a year or two. I think she arrived at Granton with a cargo of esparto grass and was then towed across to Leith for lay-up, and I seem to recall that she never sailed again and eventually went for breaking up. Salvesen's experimental freeze-at-sea trawler the *Fairfree* was also there at about that time, getting rustier and rustier (she was a converted Canadian-built minesweeper and was laid up at that berth for around five years before being towed over to Charlestown for breaking-up in the late 1950s).

On the west bank of the Water of Leith there were warehouses going right to the water's edge and no cargo berths; small ships still went to the Menzies' ship repair yard (no relation), with a small and elderly dry dock, and the entrance to the East Old Dock was still in use but only occasionally saw coasters. The swing-bridge is still there but it was fixed, and its hydraulic machinery removed, around 40 years ago.
COLIN MENZIES, 17 Bickenhall Mansions, London W1U 6BP

It's now twelve years since I first came across your magazine, and I've enjoyed reading every issue, especially when I see a picture of a ship I know something about. Such was the case with Graeme Somner's photograph of the *Amelia* on page 195 of 'Record' 56.

However, the caption statement that W. Cooper and Son 'had her from 1920 until she was broken up at Charlestown in 1955' is not completely correct. Knowing your passion for accuracy, I have to tread carefully, but the relevant publications in my book collection indicate otherwise. In their 'Days of Orkney Steam' (1971) Alastair and Anne Cormack say of the *Amelia* 'In 1920 Cooper and Sons bought the far-travelled *Amelia*... After her launching in 1894 she had spent six years on the east coast of England before emigrating to Nova Scotia. While in Canadian waters, *Amelia* was wrecked near Cape Sable, but was later salved and returned to England. From 1920 to 1955 the silhouette of *Amelia* was a familiar feature on the sea-route to Leith, although she was latterly managed, and finally absorbed into, the 'North Co.''. In his book 'The North Boats' of 1999 the late Alistair McRobb states 'Early in 1940 a third purchase was the small coasting steamer *Amelia* (built 1894) and at 357 tons gross was even smaller than the *St. Fergus*. This purchase was of a different nature [to the *St. Fergus*] in that she had been owned by Cooper and Company of Kirkwall since 1920, operating a direct Kirkwall to Leith service and the purchase was effectively a takeover of Coopers...'

I haven't any online access to check how long the ship might have remained registered in Cooper's ownership, but to all intents and purposes she was a 'North boat' for the last fifteen years of her career. She was withdrawn and scrapped after a new *St. Rognvald* came into service in 1955.

My father served as mate on most of the North Company's ships – except the *Amelia* – from June 1950 to June 1956. In Lerwick he regularly took me aboard whichever ship he happened to be on, and I can clearly remember the *Amelia* being discussed, for none of the company's officers relished a relieving stint aboard her, given her age and lack of power. The masters of North Company ships on passage used to exchange progress reports by radio telephone every night at 9 p.m.; on one occasion Captain Ramsay of the *Amelia* was heard to tell Captain Dundas of the modern twin-screw *St. Ninian* that while the poor weather might not be troubling his fine command, 'He was lucky not to be in charge of this bloody old raft in the Pentland Firth!'

Keep the Records coming!
CHARLES SIMPSON, Wilhoul, Cunningsburgh, Shetland ZE2 9HG
The registration papers for Amelia, *lodged in the National Archives at Kew, do not record a sale to the North Company. They maintain that, from June 1940 when she was sold by Peter S. Cooper until her Register was closed on sale to breakers in October 1955, she remained in the ownership of W. Cooper and Son (Kirkwall) Ltd. 'Days of Orkney Steam' notes on page 63 that '...she was latterly managed, and finally absorbed into, the 'North Co.'. In the 1955 'Mercantile Navy List',* Amelia's *manager is listed as a Robert C. Mackie, who also managed the North Company's ships.*

The explanation comes from a history of William and Peter Cooper in the papers of the late Graeme Somner, in which he records that '...by June 1940 it was no longer practical to operate a one-ship service with restrictions as to movement and times of sailings, so William Cooper and Son was bought out by its big rival, 'The North Company' for the sum of £14,000. William Cooper and Son (Kirkwall) Ltd. was formed on 21st

There were two ships named *Kaupo* under the British flag in the 1950s, and the first of these certainly had a story to tell, having worked under five different flags, and not always changing them willingly. She was built as *Alga* in 1905 by Swan, Hunter and Wigham Richardson Ltd., Newcastle to the order of owners in Trieste, for whom she would have flown the Austro-Hungarian flag. After the First World War Trieste, and the ship, became Italian, although with no change of name or owner. Sale in 1929 saw her become *Kaupo*, a name bestowed by the Kalnins family of Riga. Latvia was forced to become part of the Soviet Union in June 1940, and *Kaupo* was put under state control and the hammer and sickle. She had the misfortune to be in Lubeck on 22nd June 1941, the day Operation Barbarossa was launched against a largely unprepared (although by no means unwarned) USSR. The Germans seized her and renamed her *Westpreussen*, and she survived the war to be found by British forces at Flensburg in May 1945. The two years it took for her to be returned to service as *Kaupo* suggests she was hardly undamaged, and in June 1947 she was registered in the ownership of the Ministry of Transport, which allocated her management to Springwell Shipping Co. Ltd., in whose colours she is pictured above. Springwell and their associates had a fascinating collection of ships at this period, and the editors would be delighted to know more about them, and what if any connections they had with Eastern Europe.

In 1951 *Kaupo* was sold once more, to the Kaupo Steam Ship Co. Ltd. (C. Hoffmann and Co. Ltd., managers), London, but may have done little work, as she arrived at Dunston-on-Tyne on 29th June 1952 for breaking up by Clayton and Davie Ltd.

Colin Menzies confirms that it was the second *Kaupo* that he remembers seeing laid up at Leith, and the photograph of her below may well have been taken in the port. This steamer was delivered in September 1922 by Odense Staalskibsvaerft to an A.P. Møller company as *Betty Maersk*. She took the name *Kaupo* in 1953, in the registered ownership of the Kaupo Steam Ship Co. Ltd. (note the letter K on her funnel) which was c/o a Mrs Irma Reinhards, London, her name suggesting she was from one of the Baltic states. *Kaupo* arrived at Inverkeithing, probably under tow from Leith, on 23rd September 1959 to be broken up by T.W. Ward Ltd. *[World Ship Society Ltd.; J. and M. Clarkson collection]*

June 1940 with a share capital of £15,000 in £1 shares, with Amelia *being valued at £10,200. 'The North Company' held 13,996 shares, whilst Peter Shearer Cooper held 1,000 (plus being paid a sum of £14,000).' Ed.*

Talbot-Booth goes to war

Over the hill from us in Porthleven, Cornwall lies RNAS Culdrose, a large Royal Navy air base and home to many hundreds of serving personnel. In the early 1980s Sally Layshon, a Navy wife, was my office secretary. When her husband Brian set off for the Arabian Gulf, as chief pilot and in charge of H.M.S. *Sheffield's* flight, he happened to mention that it would be useful if his team could easily identify the merchant ships that they over-flew when on patrol. I suspected a sense of rivalry and getting one up on the bridge watch keepers. We lent Brian the office copies of Talbot-Booth.

Homeward bound H.M.S. *Sheffield* was diverted at Gibraltar to join the task force being compiled to liberate the Falkland Islands from the Argentine occupation. Inscribed in the fly leaf of the books' replacement is: *This volume replaces those generously loaned to Lieutenant Brian Leyshon on behalf of HMS* Sheffield *by Curnow Shipping Limited. The originals were on the bridge of HMS* Sheffield *and lost on 10 May 1982 when the ship sank as the result of an attack by an EXOCET missile on 4 May 1982 during the successful attempt to repel the invasion of the Falkland Islands by Argentina. Thank you for all your help.*

This was probably the first time after the conclusion of the Second World War that a Talbot-Booth work was lost during hostile enemy action.

ANDREW BELL, 'Gartul', Porthleven, Helston, Cornwall TR13 9JJ

Further copies of Talbot-Booth's magazine 'Merchant Ships' have turned up since the feature on the author's work appeared in 'Record' 56. Volume 1 ran to twelve monthly editions during 1954 and 1955, whilst there are five issues of volume 2 in the collection examined. Each issue includes several hundred drawings, in the style of later Talbot-Booth books, and the project appears to have been in lieu of a full edition of 'Merchant Ships', which appeared in 1949 but not again until 1959. Each 24-page magazine also includes black-and-white drawings of funnels, lists of sales, renamings and demolitions plus notes on model making. The editorials by Talbot-Booth (who was assisted in the first volume by Gordon A. Mills) give an insight on the great man's thoughts. He laments in one issue that subscriptions are only a quarter of those needed to sustain the operation, and only one half of those required to meet production costs. Dissatisfied readers' comments are often printed, and when these are not used the editorial laments either the state of British shipbuilding, which was beginning to lose orders to European and Japanese yards, or indeed the state of Britain itself. It would be interesting to know if volume 2 did complete its run, as

the second edition notes that a third of subscribers to volume 1 had not renewed their 25-shilling subscription. In 1955 and 1956 the World Ship Society was asking £1 for 12 issues of a similar-sized journal, albeit with considerably higher production standards. Ed.

Correcting 'Record' 12

A very belated correction to the salvage tug article in 'Record' 12. On page 256 the paragraph relating to the salvage of the *Nurtureton* has a wrong date. The *Nurtureton* was wrecked off Dungeness on 5th January 1931, not on 7th January 1932. I have just had to catalogue three negatives of the two salvaged sections when they were in the Tilbury Dry Dock and from the 'Lloyd's Weekly Casualty Reports' for the event the following dates are relevant.

5th January 1931 went ashore one and a half miles east of Dungeness in thick fog at 11 p.m. shortly before high water.
30th January 1931 ship separated into two parts by salvors.
2nd February 1931 stern section refloated at 9.30 p.m.
4th February 1931 stern section put ashore on Mucking Flats this morning by *Bullger* and *Lady Brassey*.
18th February 1931 bow section left Dungeness in tow at 7 a.m.
20th February 1931 bow section arrived at Tilbury in tow of *Bullger*, *Sun IV* and *Sun VI* at 12.35 p.m. and was taken straight into Tilbury Dock.
9th April 1931 both sections moved into Tilbury Dry Dock.
13th June 1931 both sections undocked after being made watertight and laid up at Shed 1 in Tilbury Dock.
27th May 1932 tenders being invited for repairing the *Nurtureton*, still laid up in Tilbury Dock.
8th June 1932 bow section left Tilbury in tow of tugs *Indus* and *Ebro* for Rotterdam.
9th June 1932 bow section arrived at Maassluis.
12th June 1932 stern section left Tilbury in tow of tugs *Indus* and *Ebro* for Rotterdam.
14th June 1932 stern section arrived at Maassluis.

There are no other entries in 'Lloyd's Weekly Casualty Reports' but 'Lloyd's List' shows that the *Nurtureton* sailed from the Nieuw Waterweg for Newcastle on 4th September 1932, arriving 5th September 1932.

BOB TODD, Key Specialist Curator, Historic Photographs and Ships Plans Section, National Maritime Museum, London

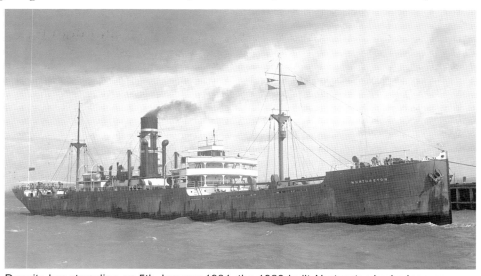

Despite her stranding on 5th January 1931, the 1929-built *Nurtureton* had a long career. She was sold out of the Chapman and Willan fleet in 1952, becoming first the German-flag *Erika Fritzen* and in 1960 renamed *Mongkok* for a final voyage to breakers in Hong Kong. [*J. and M. Clarkson*]

Loss of *Hopestar*

In Ian Rae's feature on Hopemount Shipping in 'Record' 55, page 161, he records the loss of *Hopestar* with all hands in the North Atlantic during November 1948 and the comments of the subsequent court of inquiry. Alastair Douglas kindly lent the editors a copy of the inquiry's findings, which make interesting reading.

The court of inquiry, which involved 13 days of hearings, dismissed as unlikely the possibility that *Hopestar* was overwhelmed by heavy seas, that she hit a stray mine or that she was sunk following a boiler explosion. This left the strong possibility that she broke in two because of insufficient strength. In fact, there were two alterations made which reduced the strength of *Hopestar*.

Whilst being built, and after her plans had been approved by Lloyd's Register of Shipping, her design was altered to incorporate two bunker hatches in the shelter deck. The alteration was not approved by Lloyd's Register, and neither the classification society's local surveyor nor those in its London office who saw the as-built plans appreciated that the change would affect her longitudinal strength, which was reduced to 91.6% of that required by the rules.

The second alteration was that referred to by Ian, carried out early in 1947 when the Wallsend Slipway and Engineering Co. Ltd. (a Swan Hunter subsidiary) installed a third boiler. This involved a number of alterations to *Hopestar's* structure, most seriously cutting away a substantial area of deck on each side. Recognising that this change would materially affect her longitudinal strength, the owner's Superintendent Engineer instructed the shipyard to consult Lloyd's Register about the alteration, but this was not done, possibly because of the death of the foreman responsible for the work. The court wagged its finger at this, maintaining that the owners should not have delegated this responsibility. It was calculated that these alterations, together with the changes during building, meant that *Hopestar's* longitudinal strength was now only 84.3% of that required.

Expert opinion was that, even with this reduction, *Hopestar's* strength was adequate for the voyage on which she was lost, a ballast passage from the Tyne to Philadelphia. However, she was considered too weak for the second leg of her intended voyage, when she was to load in Philadelphia for the Mediterranean. This left the court in something of a quandary:

she should not have set out on the round trip in her weakened state, yet she was considered seaworthy for the leg of the voyage on which she was actually lost. The court could not come to any definite conclusion that unseaworthiness contributed to her loss. However, it found that all concerned – owners, managers, superintendent engineers, repairers and to a minor extent Lloyd's Register – were blameworthy.

Department of correction

Thanks to Lennart Hagbjer, Ron Mapplebeck, Tore Nilsen and David Whiteside for the following notes on 'Record' 56.

Page 202: *Peronne* was renamed *Taybuoy* in 1946.

Page 217: *Aun* also carried the name *Leknes* in 1963 before becoming *Velox*.

Also on this page, the original name of the 1916-built *Ramsnes*, was *Fager* not *Falger*. *Ramsnes* was a regular visitor to UK ports, Ron Mapplebeck photographing her in Hull during July 1967 and one of the editors being delighted to encounter this veteran with a counter stern at Garston in August 1970.

Page 222: observant readers will have noticed that, although still with the funnel of A/B Transmarin, *Becky* flies the Panama flag, indicating the photograph was taken after her 1965 sale to Cia. Maritima Virona S.A., Colon, Panama (John E. Sandström & Co. A/B, Stockholm, managers) when she was presumably chartered back to her former owners.

Page 231: the delivery date of *Baron Jedburgh* was 1958.

Page 258: according to the Schell/Starke register for 1883, *Archer* was acquired by H.W. Henderson in 1891 (as stated in the caption to her photograph) and not in 1894 as in the text.

The 1916-built *Ramsnes* at Hull on July 1967. The former steamer, built at Trondhjem as *Fager*, was demolished in 1972 after a stranding. *[Ron Mapplebeck]*

SOURCES AND ACKNOWLEDGEMENTS

We thank all who gave permission for their photographs to be used, and for help in finding photographs we are particularly grateful to Tony Smith, Jim McFaul and David Whiteside of the World Ship Photo Library; to Ian Farquhar, F.W. Hawks, Peter Newall, Russell Priest, William Schell; and to David Hodge and Bob Todd of the National Maritime Museum, and other museums and institutions listed.

Research sources have included the Registers of William Schell and Tony Starke, 'Lloyd's Register', 'Lloyd's Confidential Index', 'Lloyd's Shipping Index', 'Lloyd's War Losses', 'Mercantile Navy Lists', 'Marine News', 'Sea Breezes' and 'Shipbuilding and Shipping Record'. Use of the facilities of the World Ship Society, the Guildhall Library, the National Archives and Lloyd's Register of Shipping. Particular thanks also to Heather Fenton for editorial and indexing work, and to Marion Clarkson for accountancy services.

BOSUN'S LOCKER

54/03

Apologies to David Hodge for omitting this from an earlier issue. It appears that *Cormorant* remained with William H.Tucker until 1909:

1909: Sold to James M. Stubbs, Rock Ferry.

1913: Sold to the Abel Towing Co. Ltd., Liverpool.

1922: Owners Abel Ballast and Lighterage Co. Ltd., Liverpool.

1927: Sold to William Cooper & Sons Ltd., Widnes.

24.11.1927: Registry closed and certificate cancelled, vessel broken up.

As regards her unusual position in 54/03 it would appear from a Liverpool report that on 16th February 1916 *Cormorant* was beached for an overhaul and during a heavy gale was driven against the promenade wall south of Egremont. Damage was sustained to her port bow and stem and she was making water. *Cormorant* was refloated on the 18th. The setting of the photo does not match up with any other photos taken at Egremont. However, the pier in the picture is very similar to that at Rock Ferry. Someone local to the area may be in a postition to confirm.

56/01

Writing about this photograph, which appeared on page 226 of 'Record' 54, Bob Todd has this to say: 'I cannot confirm or deny that the photograph is of the turret ship *Grindon Hall* (1908) but I do know that the *Grindon Hall*, when owned by the Leadenhall Steam Ship Co., was stranded on Salcombe Beach during a severe gale 21st October 1916. She was under the command of Captain Brewis and the entire crew was rescued. A Sidmouth resident named W.F. Yeo was awarded the Board of Trade Sea Gallantry Medal on 5th November 1916 for his part in the rescue of the crew.' Despite Bob's caution, we have no doubt that the ship depicted is indeed the *Grindon Hall*, a conclusion strengthened by comparison with the accompanying photograph of the ship (top). Note, for instance, the breaks in the bulwarks on the starboard side. Thanks also to David Whiteside for his help with this query. *[World Ship Society Ltd.]*

56/02

Christy MacHale thinks we are right that the photograph on page 226 is of

57/1

57/2

the *Memphis* of 1891. He notes that comparison with the picture of her as the *America* on page 436 of *Sea Breezes* for December 1956 leaves little doubt they are the same ship.

57/01 and 57/02

For these two photographs of a casualty from Alan Savory's collection, the question is not what ship, but

which port? She is Bullard, King's *Umvolosi* (2,986/1902), built by Laing at Sunderland and which had a long career for these owners; she was broken up at Stavanger under this name in 1930. One of the photographs has the taker's name on the back: E. Stonefield, 20 Whitby Street, West Hartlepool. Is this indeed West Hartlepool?

Pictures sometimes reach us long after the relevant article has been published. This is the case with the top photo of Elder Dempster's *Oti* aground in the Elbe. When the article in 'Record' 48, pages 195 and 200, was laid out we searched without success for an illustration of her after grounding.

In the past we have commented on photographs being altered for various reasons such as being printed in reverse to represent a sister ship. These two pictures of *San Demetrio* (8,073/1938) recently arrived in the office. We won't go into details of how the damage to the ship was sustained as so much has been written about her. Comparison of the two photographs illustrates how pictures were touched up for use in newspapers of the day, in todays parlance 'photo-shopped'. Being dark the first photograph would not have reproduced well. Retouched the damage to the ship and the messages on her would have shown up much more clearly. She also appears to have increased speed considerably.

The photographer, W. Ralston Ltd., Glasgow is credited on the back of the original. The other has details of her arriving in the Clyde on 19th November 1940, and has been rubber-stamped 'Photographic Library, Public Relations Dept., General Post Office'. One has to wonder what their interest would have been. Ralston's delivery note for the first picture was enclosed with the photos, consigning them to Eagle Oil's Shipping Department.

Mention of the Spanish Civil War in the *Telena* article reminded me of two photographs stowed away in the locker some time back but never used. They are said to have been taken at Workington in the 1930s which, considering the ships illustrated, is probably correct. Above we see *Gorbea-Mendi*, *Tom*, *Luchana* and *Margari*, all Spanish owned and registered at Bilbao. By the time the second photo was taken the order has changed and we now have *Arichachu*, a new arrival, registered at San Sebastian, *Tom*, *Gorbea-Mendi*, *Margari* and *Luchana*. *Luchana*, loaded in the first picture, is now alongside and *Tom* has been discharged. My assumption is that once discharged the vessels hoped to stay there for the duration of the Civil War or until suitable safe lay-up berths could be found elswhere. From the table below it can be seen that three of the ships had long lives, one became a war loss and one was taken out of commnercial service during the Second World War.

Name, ex names	Gross tons, built, at	Owner	Fate
Arichachu	3,812 1920 Cadiz	Cia. Naviera 'Easo' (Areizaga & Larrea - changed to Credito de la Union Minera in 8.1937 when owners went over to Nationalists).	*1939*: r/n *Gayarre* (Sp). *1967*: r/n *Astillero* (Sp). *1976*: Removed from 'Lloyd's Confidential Index'. Reported in 1988 by Lloyd's Register as having been broken up.
Tom ex *Cramond* 1921, launched as *War Moon*.	3,052 1919 Leith	Cia. Naviera Bachi (Hijos de Astigarraga).	*5.8.1937*: Captured by Nationalist armed trawlers in Bay of Biscay and taken into Bilbao. *1954*: r/n *Archanda*. *19.1.1960*: Wrecked north east of Boa Vista Island, Cape Verde.
Gorbea-Mendi	4,291 1913 Bilbao	Cia. Naviera Sota y Aznar.	*1937-1939*: Laid up at Londonderry during Civil War. *1939*: r/n *Monte Moncayo* (Sp). *28.9.1940*: Torpedoed and sunk, or may have struck a mine, about 22 miles from Capo Carbonara, Sardinia.
Margari ex *Orbe* 1928, ex *Wye Crag* 1925, ex *War Crag* 1919.	3,110 1918 West Hartlepool	Cia. Naviera Amaya (C.de Zabala).	*1937*: r/n *Redstone* (Br). *2.5.1940*: Scuttled by The Admiralty as a blockship at Scapa Flow. *1948*: Refloated and broken up at Cairnryan by W.H. Arnott Young and Co. Ltd.
Luchana ex *Oquendo* 1921, ex *Tuscany* 1914, laid down as *Lugano*.	3,000 1908 West Hartlepool	Cia. Vasco-Cantabrica de Navegacion (under Republican control during Civil War).	*1938*: Laid up at Bergen until the end of the Civil War. *1939*: r/n *Mar Tirreno* (Sp) *1955*: r/n *Muni* (Sp) *4.3.1963*: Arrived Castellon to be broken up.

PHOTOS FROM THE FYLDE
John Clarkson

The Fylde is best described as the land stretching from the rivers Ribble in the south to the Wyre in the north and from the Irish Sea in the west to, let's say, the old A6 road in the east which trundles up through Lancashire from Preston to Lancaster and beyond.

Starting in the south, ignoring Preston, there was the shipyard at Lytham, next the piers at Lytham, St.Annes and Blackpool which had numerous pleasure sailings in the summers of the first half of the twentieth century. Furthest north was Fleetwood with its fishing industry, passenger sailings along the coast to Morecambe, Heysham and Barrow, plus regular ferry services to Ireland and the Isle of Man. In the early 1900s the dock thrived on fishing, grain and timber. Coasters passing up-river to load or discharge at the I.C.I. works were a regular feature, sometimes waiting on the railway jetty at Fleetwood until there was sufficient water to proceed up river. Sadly the port is now only a shadow of what it used to be, even the Irish ferries have finished leaving a deserted ramp, a marina and inshore fishing craft.

I hope the following small collection of photographs will illustrate some of the ships and events from the first 40 years of the last century. Perhaps some of our readers will have other photographs from the area to share with us.

The Lytham-built tug *George Livesey* (110/1929) sets out from Preston on 12th March 1929 on her delivery voyage to the Thames. Some of the ships built at Lytham went up to Preston to be prepared for their coastwise voyage. Others were taken to Preston soon after their launch for boilers and other heavy engine parts to be lifted on board. They were then taken back to Lytham for their final fitting out. The builder, the Lytham Shipbuilding and Engineering Co. Ltd., was set up in 1904 and dissolved in 1957. In that time they built over nine hundred craft ranging from barges to tugs, coasters, small naval auxilliary craft and vessels for service on overseas rivers and inland waterways. *[Harry Stewart/J. and M. Clarkson]*

Michael Murphy's *Rosaleen* (409/1908) was driven ashore at St. Annes on 5th November 1911. The Lytham, Southport and Blackpool lifeboats turned out and the crew of eleven men was rescued by the Blackpool boat. According to a message on the card this picture was taken on 8th December during an unsuccessful attempt to refloat her. *Rosaleen* had been built at Dublin and although her owner was a Dublin man his ship was registered at Cardiff. Eventually refloated, she was renamed *Ita* in 1920 and *Kyle Prince* in 1934, and was wrecked near Holyhead in October 1938. *[Unless shown otherwise all illustrations in this article are from the collection of J. and M. Clarkson]*

The next ship was not so lucky. H.M.S. *Foudroyant* was an 80-gun, second rate completed in the Plymouth dockyard in 1798. She was Admiral Nelson's flagship from 1799 to 1801, later serving as a guardship and later still a training ship before being sold out of the Royal Navy in 1892 to a J. Read of Portsmouth. She was then sold on to German breakers but the public outcry was such that *Foudroyant* was bought by Mr. Wheatley Cobb for use as a training ship. The cost of restoration was so high that she was put on show in various ports around the country to raise funds. After being on display at Southport the ship was put to an anchor off Blackpool. Caught by a gale her cable parted and *Foudroyant* was driven ashore on 16th June 1897 becoming a total loss. Attempts were made to refloat her but she broke up in a gale in December of that year. Many souvenirs were made by local craftsmen from her wreckage.

The three pleasure steamers alongside the North Pier at Blackpool in 1882 are (left to right) *Great Britain, Roses* and *Queen of the Bay* (2). Blackpool had the largest number of excursion steamers in the area. *Great Britain* (200/1876), a Renfrew-built paddle steamer, was owned by the Jolliffes, a Liverpool family of tug owners. *Roses* (124/1876), nearest to the camera, was owned by Robert Birkett of Morecambe and would have come down from there on a day trip. She was registered at Lancaster. Lastly *Queen of the Bay* (2) (189/1874) belonged to the Blackpool, Lytham and Southport Steam Packet Company, Preston, where she had been built and registered.

Bickerstaffe (213/1879) was owned by John and Robert Bickerstaffe and later H.D. Bickerstaffe. In 1895 her owners became the Blackpool Passenger Steamboat Co.Ltd. Completed by Lairds at Birkenhead in 1879 the iron paddle steamer ran from Blackpool for almost fifty years before going to Garston in December 1928 to be broken up. Was the diver, right, trying to catch the boat?

The first owner of *Queen of the Bay* (2) (189/1874) was the Blackpool, Lytham and Southport Steam Packet Co. Ltd. In 1881 she was sold to the Blackpool Pier Company and in 1891 back to her builder, William Allsup and Sons Ltd. at Preston. They kept her for three years, selling her in 1894 to the Goole and Hull Steam Towing Co. Ltd. at Goole. *Queen of the Bay* (2) remained with them until 1917, retaining her Preston registration, which was closed in April, 1917 on her sale to the War Office.

The iron paddle steamer *Wellington* (137/1871) was completed at Preston in 1871 by Allsups for Robert Bickerstaffe of Blackpool. In 1894 she went to the South Blackpool Jetty Co. Ltd. and in 1895 to the Blackpool Passenger Steamboat Co. Ltd. Her registration was transferred from Preston to Fleetwood in 1896 although 'Lloyd's Register' continued to show Preston. *Wellington* was reported in July 1913 to have been broken up.

The Fleetwood registered *Belle* (147/1892), launched as *Llandudno Belle*, was built of steel by Willoughby Brothers Ltd. at Plymouth. Owned by the North Pier Steamship Co. (Blackpool) Ltd., *Belle* came to Blackpool in about 1895 for Blackpool to Southport sailings. Her Fleetwood registration was closed in 1924 and the note 'vessel broken up Bo'ness August, 1923' added. *[Roy Fenton collection]*

Sleek maybe, but not really attractive, although beauty is always in the eye of the beholder, *Queen of the North* (590/1895) was another product of Laird's yard at Bikenhead. Built for the Blackpool Passenger Steamboat Co. Ltd., she ran to Douglas, Isle of Man. Hired by the Admiralty in March 1916 for minesweeping duties, *Queen of the North* was mined and sunk off Orfordness on 20th July 1917.

The summer of 1937 was the only one when *Atalanta, Minden* and *Queen of the Bay* (3) all sailed from Blackpool. *Atalanta* (top) (486/1906) was completed in 1906 on Clydebank for the Glasgow and South Western Railway. The Blackpool Steam Navigation Co. Ltd. bought her in March 1937 for their longer runs - those to Barrrow and Llandudno. *Atalanta* was the last steamer in the fleet. In the Second World War she served at Rosyth and Scapa Flow after which she was not refitted but sent for scrap in 1945.

Minden (533/1903) (middle) was built at Londonderry as the Mersey ferry *Bidston*. Prior to her purchase by Blackpool Pleasure Steamers Ltd. in June 1933 she had held the name *Old Bidston* for a very short period. Replaced by *Atalanta* late in 1937, *Minden* was transferred to the Blackpool Steam Navigation Co. Ltd. in 1938 and sold for breaking up at Preston in October of that year. When first purchased she sailed with a buff funnel. A black top was added later as shown right.

The twin-screw *Queen of the Bay* (3) (783/1919) (bottom) was completed in 1919 by W. Simons and Co. Ltd., Renfrew. Laid down as a minesweeper she was finished as the survey vessel H.M.S. *Crozier*. Before then two other names had been mooted - *Ventnor* and *Verwood*. Soon after being delivered, *Crozier* was sold to South Africa and in 1922 was renamed *Protea*. Bought by Blackpool Pleasure Steamers Ltd., *Protea* arrived back in the United Kingdom in December 1935 after a stormy 98-day passage. She passed to the Blackpool Steam Navigation Co. Ltd. in May 1936 and was renamed *Queen of the Bay*. Shown here with her hull white, this was later changed to black. In 1936 and 1937 she operated on the Blackpool to Llandudno service and was sold in October 1937 to French and later Spanish buyers. Sunk by Nationalists in the Spanish Civil War she was later raised and served as a training ship until going for breaking up in 1950. [*B. and A.Feilden/Roy Fenton collection*]

Fleetwood, situated on the Wyre, is well-known for its involvement in the fishing industry which is now, sadly, almost a thing of the past. All that remains is a fleet of mainly inshore vessels. Wyre Dock was completed in 1877 and the Fish Dock, accessed though Wyre Dock, was added later. The pier at Fleetwood, from where many wives watched their husbands sail for the fishing grounds, opened in 1910 and was the last new pier to be constructed in the United Kingdom. Following a fire in September 2008 the pier was demolished. The impressive railway station of 1883 closed in 1966 and was later demolished.

Our first Fleetwood photograph is of two United Alkali vessels, *Davy* (99/1891) and *Leblanc* (109/1891), in Wyre Dock along with the Fleetwood registered schooner *Lancashire Lad* (151/1870). The schooner was owned by Porter's Shipping Co. Ltd., Fleetwood and had been built at nearby Glasson Dock. On 2nd February 1903 *Lancaster Lad* was wrecked in Scrabster Roads, Thurso Bay whilst on passage from the Mersey to Morrishaven with coal. *Leblanc* and *Davy* were both owned by the United Alkali Co. Ltd. of Liverpool. Sister ships, they had a third sister *Faraday* (102/1891). All had been built down the coast at Lytham to dimensions suitable for entering the Old Dock at Widnes. The three were mainly employed in carrying limestone from North Wales quarries to the Burn Naze works further up the Wyre. *Leblanc* was sold in 1918 and carried general cargoes from the Mersey to Conway and Menai, later passing to Irish owners. In due course *Davy* went to Abels of Liverpool for the ballast trade and finally rotted away at Widnes. The completion dates of *Davy* and *Leblanc*, along with the loss of the schooner, place the date of this photo between 1891 and 1903.

Seen berthing on the railway berth, *Indium* (207/1923) was also owned by the United Alkali Co. Ltd., later Imperial Chemical Industries Ltd. *Indium* and others in the fleet were used to bring limestone to Burn Naze and to take away soda ash for use in industry and for export. Sometimes there would be insufficient water to reach Burn Naze, congestion on the berth or a wait for cargo in which case they would lie alongside the railway berth near to the station in Fleetwood. *Indium* had a long life, latterly as a sand pump, and was finally broken up on the Tyne in 1963.

The twin-screw *Wyvern* (215/1905) was built by Ferguson Brothers at Port Glasgow for the Midland Railway Company, later passing to the London, Midland and Scottish Railway. Essentially a tug, she was also used for excursions, on this occasion to carry holiday makers to the Heysham Tower Camp. Her end came in March 1960 when she went to P. Mulholland and Sons at Millom, Cumbria for breaking up.

In the early days of the twentieth century Fleetwood was an important embarkation point for Ireland with sailings to Belfast and Londonderry. The Lancashire and Yorkshire and London and North Western Railway was famous for its fleet of 'Dukes' represented here by the twin-screw, Clydebank-built *Duke of Connaught* (1,564/1892) seen sailing from Fleetwood (top). Sailings continued throughout the war although on one occasion she was shelled by a U-boat but managed to escape. 1923 saw her transferred to the London, Midland and Scottish Railway's Heysham to Douglas route. Later working on the east coast, in May 1934 *Duke of Connaught* was sold for breaking up in the Netherlands.

The Isle of Man Steam Packet Co. Ltd. commenced sailings from Fleetwood in 1876 and continued through to 1961 after which there were intermittent sailings. Other operators at times tried to run similar services. The twin-screw *Rushen Castle* (1,724/1898), seen right, built by Vickers at Barrow began her days running out of Fleetwood as the *Duke of Cornwall*. In 1923 she was transferred to the London, Midland and Scottish Railway's Heysham to Douglas route. When the Fleetwood services ended in 1928 *Duke of Cornwall* was bought by the Steam Packet, modernised and renamed *Rushen Castle*. She lasted until 1947 when she went to Belgian breakers.

Not to be ignored is the little *Wyresdale* (54/1924), the Knott End ferry (bottom) which was built at Fleetwood and owned by Fleetwood Urban District Council. She served the short route until 1957 when a boiler explosion killed three people and she was taken out of service. Thought to have been broken up soon after, she was later noted at Glasson Dock but her ultimate fate is not known.

In the early part of the 20th century the Furness Railway Company ran sailings between Barrow and Fleetwood. Their four main ships were the *Lady Margaret* (369/1895), *Lady Evelyn* (342/1900) and *Lady Moyra* (519/1905) (top) along with the short-lived General Steam Navigation vessel *Philomel* (564/1889). *Lady Moyra* was formerly the Bristol Channel paddle steamer *Gwalia*, built by J. Brown and Co. Ltd. at Glasgow.

The blue-hulled *Lady Moyra* operated across Morecambe Bay until the First World War. Hired by the Admiralty in November 1915 for service as a minesweeper, she was returned to her owners in July 1919 and sold soon after to P. and A. Campbell Ltd. Renamed *Brighton Queen* in 1933 she was lost at Dunkirk on 31st May 1940. *[Ian Boyle collection]*

No item about Fleetwood would be complete without a steam trawler such as *Admiral Sir John Lawford* (338/1930), completed by Smith's Dock at Stockton-on-Tees in 1930 for the Iago Steam Trawler Co. Ltd., registered at London, coal-fired and designed for fishing in Icelandic waters. In 1958 she was sold to the Milford Steam Trawling Co. Ltd. and renamed *Milford Admiral*. However, her end was near and on 8th January 1962 she arrived in Ward's yard at Briton Ferry to be broken up.

Our last picture, again a trawler but one not so lucky, is of *Commandant Bultinck* (219/1911), another product of Smith's Dock at Stockton. Built for T.G. Hancock of Milford Haven as the *Marloes* she was sold to Hesketh Steam Trawlers Ltd., retaining her name but re-registered at Fleetwood with the fishing number FD170. Resold to Belgian buyers in the late 1920s, she became *Commandant Bultinck*. On the 2nd October 1929 after fishing off the Isle of Man she was swept ashore at Rossall, near Fleetwood. Three Belgian crew members were lost whilst attempting to reach the shore to get help. The vessel became a total loss and was broken up in situ.